GIVE ME SHELTER

Give Me Shelter copyright © Frances Lincoln Limited 2007
Text copyright © Tony Bradman and the authors as named 2007

front cover photo REUTERS/Damir Sagolj

First published in Great Britain and in the USA in 2007 by
Frances Lincoln Children's Books, 4 Torriano Mews,
Torriano Avenue, London NW5 2RZ

www.franceslincoln.com

First paperback published in Great Britain in 2009

A catalogue record for this book is available from the British Library.

ISBN: 978-1-84780-002-2

Printed and bound in Great Britain by CPI Bookmaque, Croydon, Surrey in May 2011

3 5 7 9 8 6 4 2

GIVE ME SHELTER

Stories about children who seek asylum
edited by Tony Bradman

FRANCES LINCOLN
CHILDREN'S BOOKS

"Exceptional. Children who read [these] stories will see their world afresh and understand it better."
School Librarian

"A seriously important book."
Books for Keeps (four stars)

"A timely book."
Carousel

"An eye-opening collection, which will hopefully evoke empathy and understanding amongst all who read it."
Booktrust Children's Books

"The Frances Lincoln list represents a veritable treasure trove of world views, belief systems and personalities. *Give Me Shelter* is the undisputed jewel within this crown. Here is a book that should be made universally available as a declaration of care and compassion in every bookshop, library, school and home across the land."
Achuka

Contents

Acknowledgements

I would like to thank Arts Council England for their support. Their grant made it possible for me as a busy freelancer to spend the time I needed to find just the right people to contribute to this anthology. Charles Beckett at the Arts Council England office in London was particularly helpful.

I'd also like to thank Janetta Otter-Barry at Frances Lincoln for having the vision to commission *Give Me Shelter*, and also my editor, Gemma Rochelle for all her hard work, organisational skills and support. And thanks must also go yet again to my exemplary agent, Hilary Delamere. And last but not least, I'd like to thank all the writers for your hard work and patience. Your stories have taught me more than I can say!

Introduction

I can remember exactly where I was and what I was doing when I first got the idea for this book. I was sitting on the sofa one winter evening, watching television. My wife and I had eaten a good supper, and I had that relaxed end-of-the-day, everything-is-fine kind of feeling. Just like millions of others at that moment in our rich, safe country, I'm sure.

Then the news came on, and that feeling soon began to fade. It was the usual catalogue of gloom. Among other things, there were problems at a place called Sangatte, near Calais in France. A camp there was being used to hold people seeking asylum in Britain. Conditions were bad, there were escape attempts, and it was all causing a great deal of controversy.

One image in particular struck me. There was a film of asylum-seekers climbing the fences around the entrance to the Channel Tunnel, and for a moment the camera lingered on a young boy. He didn't look any older than eight or nine, and yet there he was, on his own, probably hundreds of miles from home, doing something incredibly dangerous to get into Britain.

Of course, to many people in Britain – and in other rich, safe countries – that small boy is a big problem. Headlines in newspapers scream about Britain 'being swamped' by asylum-seekers. Some politicians claim that many of them aren't fleeing from war or persecution and shouldn't be allowed in, and as a result there is fear and resentment and hatred.

But I wanted to know where that small boy had come from. Few people leave their homes and their families unless they're forced to. So what had brought him to that moment? What had happened to his family? What terrible events had uprooted him from the place where was born and sent him to that moment of danger, poised on a fence in France?

I'll probably never know the truth of that boy's story. But as I was sitting there watching TV, I realised I could make it possible for other stories to be told, stories that would reveal what lay behind the headlines. I decided I would try to put together a collection of short stories about asylum-seekers and even, if possible, by asylum-seekers themselves.

And so *Give Me Shelter* came into being. It took me a while to find writers who could bring alive the experience of being an asylum-seeker, but I did it in the end. The stories are about people from all over the world – Kosovo, Eritrea, Vietnam, Zimbabwe.

They're fiction, but they're grounded in reality. Some of the writers have been asylum-seekers, while others have worked with people who have been in that position.

I hope that reading them will help us understand what it means to be an asylum-seeker – to be forced to leave your home and seek the comfort of strangers. And that some day, boys like the one I saw on TV won't have to climb fences. Or if he does, that we will be happy to give him shelter...

Baa and the Angels
by Nicki Cornwell

This is a story about a family who get caught up in the civil war in the Democratic Republic of Congo, a country in the middle of Africa. When there's a civil war, the citizens of a country fight each other, and innocent people who want to lead happy, peaceful lives get drawn into the violence. This is what leads them to seek asylum. The story takes place in 1999. Since 2003 there has been a fragile peace.

"Hurry!" Sabine urges her sister.

Seven year old Thérèse is dawdling. She is watching the children who don't go to school. They don't wear school uniform or carry rucksacks. They wear patched clothes and carry large, yellow jerry cans. They are going to the river to fetch water.

Sabine is fuming. If only she could leave Thérèse behind! But she is nine, she is the big sister. Baba insists that they should walk to school together because of them. Baba's voice becomes an angry hiss when he talks about *them*. Beads of sweat gather on his forehead, and Mama's eyes become wide and frightened like those of a cornered antelope.

"What do *they* look like?" Sabine ventures to ask.

Baba picks up an overripe mango. "They are

10

like this mango! *They* look all right on the outside, but inside they are rotten all through! And there's a stone for a heart. See?"

He flings the mango out of the door. It splits open, spilling the rotting flesh on the ground. "That's what *they're* like! The Congo is full of *them*. The Congo is getting torn apart!"

Night time, when it is dark, is the time when Sabine is most afraid of *them*, but even going to school is scary. She keeps a close watch on the shadows behind the houses in case one of them is hiding there. She looks out for snakes, too, but she is much more afraid of *them*.

The sun is climbing the sky, scorching the ground and sizzling the branches of the avocado trees.

"Hurry!" cries Sabine.

Soon she is near enough to the school to hear the usual sounds of children waiting for lessons to begin: laughing, shouting, and the dull thud of shoes against the battered football. But everything is quiet. Lessons must have started, but if that is the case, why can't she hear the teacher's deep voice and the chanting responses of the children?

She forgets Thérèse, she begins to run. Now she can see the school building, with its wrinkled tin roof spread over white-painted walls. She pulls up with a jerk, Thérèse close behind her. Sabine hears strange, unfamiliar sounds – strident, guttural shouts. A desk flies out of the school and lands on the worn earth. Papers spill out on to the ground.

Suddenly a harsh cry slices through the air. A hard-faced man with a gun tucked in his belt strides towards them.

"Hey, you! You want school?"

Sabine feels a lightning stab of fear. She grabs hold of Thérèse and bolts. There is a loud bang. Something flies past Sabine's ears and rustles through the trees.

Mocking laughter rings through the air.

"I'll give you school!"

◇ ◇ ◇

Sabine and Thérèse don't stop running till they get back home. Mama is outside, hanging the washing on the bushes, with the six scrawny hens pecking at her feet. No sooner do they hear the children coming than the hens scatter with a wild clucking and flapping.

The children hurl themselves into Mama's arms.

Mama cries, "What's wrong?"

"There are soldiers in the school. A man shouted at us. He had a gun," pants Sabine.

Mama's face quivers with fear. She pulls them into the house and pushes the door shut. She collapses on to the bench and holds the two children as if she will never let them go.

Four-year-old Lou looks up. She is feeding her doll with *ugali*.

"Biny!" she cries. "Help me feed Baa!"

Baa is a *mzungu* doll. Her eyes are blue, and her skin is the colour of a cloth that has been bleached by the sun. A *mzungu* who fell into one of the ponds at the fish farm gave Baba the doll, because Baba rescued him. The doll is supposed to be for all the children, but Lou always gets Baa because she makes such a big fuss if she doesn't.

Sabine is feeling as if someone has shaken her up and down. She would love to have a cuddle with Baa, but she doesn't dare ask. She is afraid that Lou will say no!

"Baa needs a wash!" she tells Lou. "She's got *ugali* all over her face!"

"Yes!" nods Lou. "Baa needs a wash. You help me, Biny!"

Sabine helps Lou. That way she has a chance of holding Baa, if only for a minute or two.

◇ ◇ ◇

Baba comes home early. His face lights up with relief when he sees the children. He can't stop hugging them.

"Guess what!" cries Thérèse. "There are soldiers in our school!"

"I heard about that!" says Baba.

"What about the teacher?" says Mama.

"*They* are looking for him," Baba says wearily. "*They* are saying he's a terrorist."

"Lies, all lies!" said Mama angrily. "The teacher is a good man!"

"What's a terrorist?" asks Sabine.

"Someone who does bad things," says Baba. "Those soldiers, they are the real terrorists. You kids will have to stay near the house for the next few days. Things aren't safe at the moment."

Sabine feels her stomach turn over. She snuggles up to Mama.

"*They* are in the village now," says Baba. He gives a deep sigh. "There will be no stopping *them*."

The neighbours are frightened, too. No one goes far from their houses, and everyone is jumpy and scared. Sabine begins to feel as if someone has locked her up in a cage. She misses school badly, especially singing in the choir.

◇ ◇ ◇

The big rains start. One day Sabine hears a harsh rattling sound that she hasn't heard before. The rattling stops and starts, stops and starts. Then there is an eerie silence as if all the living things in the trees are holding their breath.

Baba and Mama exchange nervous glances.

"What was that?" cries Sabine.

"Gunfire," says Baba. "Big guns. It's okay, they're a long way off!" He tries to smile, but his smile is forced.

"I don't like it!" cries Lou. "Make it stop!"

"I can't," says Baba.

Baba doesn't go to work that day. He doesn't go to market. He stays at home.

The guns go on crackling for what seems like a long time. Then they stop. Everything goes quiet. Sabine finds the silence scary.

◇ ◇ ◇

Next day, Baba goes off to work as usual. Soon after he goes, the crackle of guns begins. The sound is nearby. Sabine lifts the cloth and peeps out of the window. People are running past the house, their faces full of fear. There are shouts – and shots.

"Stay away from that window!" snaps Mama.

Suddenly there is an enormous bang. The house shakes. The candle falls off the table and rolls over the floor. Didi startles away from Mama's breast and begins to scream. Thérèse and Lou scuttle to hide in Mama's skirts.

"Come here, kids!" screams Mama. She rushes into the bedroom. The children bolt after her. Mama crouches down in the corner. The children huddle against her. Mama drags a cover over them all.

15

Sabine is terrified. It is hot under the cover. She can hardly breathe.

"I want my Baa!" cries Lou.

"Ssh!" hissed Mama.

They wait.

Then they hear footsteps, urgent footsteps.

Someone runs into the house!

A voice cries, "Celeste?"

"It's Baba Paul!" cries Mama. "We're in here, Paul!"

Mama emerges from her hiding-place, clutching Didi. Sabine and Thérèse cling to her wrap. They are too frightened to let go. Lou makes a quick dive for Baa and hurtles back to Mama. They are all clinging on to each other.

Baba Paul is shaking and shivering. Sweat beads his forehead. Blood swells out of a gash on his cheek.

"*They* got your man!" he gasps.

"What?"

Baba Paul shakes his head. He makes the sign of the Cross.

Mama goes stony still.

"What am I going to do?" she cries. Tears begin to roll down her cheeks.

The children cower into her wrap.

"Go to Father Jacob, that's what your man said! He'll tell you what to do!" cries Baba Paul, his voice hoarse and exhausted.

"Leave my home?" cries Mama.

"You'll be dead if you don't!" cries Baba Paul. "*They*'ll be after you and the kids now!"

"What about you?"

Baba Paul gives a ghastly smile. "I'm staying. I'll hide out for while. Someone's got to look after our mother!"

Mama nods. The tears stream down her face.

"I'll go to the fish farm and see if they'll lend me a jeep," says Baba Paul. "It's the only way you'll get there!"

Mama puts her hands over her face. She begins to rock. Sabine feels quivers of fear in her chest. She pulls at Mama's sleeve and says, "Mama, what's happening?"

Mama takes her hands away from her face.

"We're going to run away from this stupid old war!" she says. Tears are still rolling down her cheeks. "We'll go to another country and come back when it's over!"

"But what about Baba? We can't leave him behind!"

"Baba's already gone!" says Mama. Her voice is tight. "He's gone to live with the angels! Give your sisters some water and *ugali* while I bundle up a few bits! Hurry now, child!"

"Yes, Mama!"

Sabine knows that something bad has happened to Baba, but living with the angels doesn't sound like a bad thing. Her head feels as if it is bursting, there is so much muddle inside it, but she doesn't dare ask any more questions.

Mama puts the baby down on the bed. She takes money from a bag and hides it in a pocket under her skirt. She pulls clothes out of drawers and throws them on to the bed.

"Lou! Put your Baa in the bundle!" she says.

"I don't want to!" cries Lou.

"You can't carry her, she'll get lost!"

Lou's face screws up, but she lets Mama take Baa. Mama ties up the bundle. Baa disappears from sight.

Sabine says, "Aren't you going to eat anything, Mama?"

"Yes, child!"

Mama sits down by Sabine. She is breathing heavily and she smells of fear. She breaks pieces off the *ugali* and pushes them into her mouth.

◇ ◇ ◇

When Baba Paul comes back, he is driving a battered old jeep. He throws the bundle into the back and they all squeeze in beside him. Didi is wrapped against Mama's chest, leaving both hands free to hold Lou and Thérèse against her. Sabine just fits in by the window.

The jeep draws away from the house. Mama

sniffs. Sabine's stomach has tied itself in knots. She keeps turning to look back at the road. She is sure that *they* will follow.

On and on they go, over a rough, rutted track. A fierce sun is roasting the jeep and everything inside it. Soon there are damp patches on Baba Paul's shirt, and Mama keeps wiping her face and fanning the air with an old piece of cardboard. Every time Sabine shifts her position she has to peel away her legs from the seat. One by one they fall asleep, all except Baba Paul who is driving the car and Mama who stares out of the window and watches the trees pass by with unseeing eyes.

Sabine wakes up when the car stops. Strong arms reach into the car and carry her into a building. She hears Mama's voice, she hears Baba Paul's voice, she is laid down on a mat and she goes back to sleep.

◇ ◇ ◇

When Sabine wakes up, sunlight is pouring through the window.

Mama is talking to a priest. He is giving Mama papers and money.

"That should get you out of the country," he says. "When you get to the new country, tell them who you are and ask for asylum."

He says a quick prayer and makes the sign of the

Cross. "May God protect you!"

Thérèse and Lou are still asleep. Baba Paul carries them out and puts them into the jeep next to Mama and Didi. Sabine just manages to pull herself up and climb into the jeep. Baba Paul shuts the door behind her. She collapses against Thérèse and goes to sleep again.

After a while she wakes up and slowly peels herself away from Thérèse. The jeep is lurching over the ground on a track that has so many holes in it, Baba Paul has to keep swerving from side to side. Soon Thérèse and Lou wake up, too.

"Are we nearly there?" asks Thérèse.

"Not yet," says Baba Paul.

"Where are we going?"

"You're going on an aeroplane."

"An aeroplane?" The children are wonder-struck and silent.

The sun sinks lower in the sky. Suddenly Baba Paul brakes the car.

"There's the turn. I almost missed it!"

He backs the jeep down the track and swings off to the left. A few minutes later, the track ends in the bumpy grass of an airstrip. A small plane is waiting for them, its engine already running. It doesn't look big enough to hold them all.

Baba Paul draws up beside the plane and helps them out. He hugs each one of them and gives Mama some money.

"Take this," he says. "I wish I had more."

"Take care of our mother," says Mama. Her eyes are bright with tears. Sabine feels her eyes prickle and her chest grows tight.

A thin, scared-looking man pokes his head out of the plane and holds his hands out. Baba Paul throws the bundle up to him.

"That's the pilot," says Baba Paul.

The sky darkens. Night is almost there. They are just lifting Sabine when another jeep drives up and skids to a halt by the plane, headlights flooding the grass. Paralyzed with fear, she clings to Baba Paul.

"It's *them*!" she screams.

"No, no, it's not *them*!" cries Baba Paul.

Two men and a woman get out. One of the men has his arm bandaged up. The other has to be carried to the plane. The driver throws a couple of bundles up to the pilot and backs the jeep away. The pilot switches on the headlights and revs up the engine. Didi starts to cry.

"He doesn't like the noise," says Mama.

"Where's my Baa?" Lou says anxiously.

Mama says, "Don't worry! She's in the bundle!"

Baba Paul can just be seen in the headlights of the plane. He waves and backs away.

The plane leaves the ground and begins to climb into the sky. At first Sabine is scared, but after a while she gets used to the bumpy, jolting movement.

Her eyes feel heavy, she wants to cuddle up to

Mama, but Mama has the baby in her arms, and Thérèse and Lou have fallen asleep on each side of her. There is nowhere for Sabine. She looks out at the never-ending sky and thinks of the angels she has seen in a book at school.

"Where do angels live?" she asks Mama.

"In heaven," Mama says, looking out at the sky. A tear rolls down her cheek.

"Is that where Baba is? When is he coming back?"

Mama doesn't answer straight away. When she does, her voice is sad. She says, "Baba's not coming back, child."

"Did Baba get hurt?" Sabine asks fearfully. "Did the bad men hurt him?"

"Yes. But Baba's all right now," says Mama. "The angels will take care of him! Hush, child, get some sleep like your sisters!"

◇ ◇ ◇

When the plane lands, it is dark. The pilot helps the passengers to climb down from the plane. Mama goes first, with Didi tied to her back. The sleepy children are passed down to her, one after another, and the bundles are thrown to the ground. Then everyone climbs into a waiting truck.

The truck stops in front of an enormous building with lots of windows and lots of lights shining out of them. Sabine has never seen so many lights before.

"Wait!" says the driver of the truck. "I'll get you a trolley!"

Mama loads the bundle, Thérèse and Lou on to the trolley. Sabine has to walk. Inside the building there are lots of people, some walking busily, others sitting and standing around. Sabine sees two men in uniforms talking to each other. Their skins are the colour of a dead chicken when all the feathers had been plucked from it.

"Mama!" she whispers, tugging at her mother's arm, "Look at those men! They are *mzungus*, aren't they!"

"Don't point, Sabine, it's rude!" says Mama. "Yes, they are white people. They can't help being like that. That's the way they're born."

Mama wheels the children round on the trolley and talks to lots of men in uniforms, many of whom are *mzungus*. Sabine keeps well away from them. She has often been told that if she doesn't behave, they will carry her away!

They wait in a queue. When they get to the front, the woman checks Mama's bundle.

"Baa!" shrieks Lou, as Baa's head appears.

"Not now, Lou!" says Mama as she ties up the bundle again. "You can have Baa later!"

She hands the bundle to a man standing by a machine. He wraps the bundle round and round in blue skin, pulls a sticker in half, slaps one piece on the bundle and hands the other to Mama. Then he loads the bundle on to a trolley and wheels it away.

"Baa!" shrieks Lou as the trolley disappears.

"It's all right, Lou!" soothes Mama. "He'll give us back the bundle when we get to the UK."

"The UK?" says Sabine. A little sprig of excitement begins to take root in her heart.

"Is that where we're going?"

"Yes," says Mama sadly. "I wish we were going to France! No one's going to speak any of our languages in the UK. I won't understand anything they say!"

The airport is emptying. Those who have nowhere to go are settling down for the night. Mama still has some *ugali*, and she manages to buy a bottle of milk from a bar that is still open. The children eat hungrily. There is only just enough food. Then they find a quiet corner and fall asleep on each other, curled up like a heap of puppies.

"Baa! I want Baa! " Lou whimpers as she drifts off to sleep.

◇ ◇ ◇

In the morning, Mama counts up her money.

"There's not much left," she sighs, "but God will provide!"

The airport is filling up again. People keep

arriving with their suitcases, bags and bundles.

Mama shows her papers to a man in a uniform. Then they follow everyone else out into the full heat of the sun. And there stands the biggest plane that Sabine has ever seen. It is so big that there are lots of steps up to the door.

A *mzungu* helps them to find their seats. She speaks French, and she has blue eyes and hair the colour of fire. Pinned to her chest is a badge saying 'Angie'.

The plane starts to growl. The growling grows louder.

The plane takes off. It climbs higher and higher until it flies through the clouds.

"Are we nearly in heaven?" asks Sabine.

"Certainly not!" said Mama. "Whatever put that idea into your head?"

Mama starts to feed Didi. Didi sucks and cries, sucks and cries. Something is wrong.

"Why is Didi crying?" asks Sabine.

"I haven't got enough milk for him," says Mama.

Angie appears at Mama's side. She says, "Would you like a bottle for him?"

Mama nods gratefully.

Angie brings a bottle and a packet of nappies for Didi. She also brings packets of crisps for the three girls.

"You're an angel!" says Mama.

"Do angels fly in aeroplanes?" says Sabine in surprise.

"Of course they do!" says Mama.

Was Baba flying round the world in an aeroplane full of angels? Was that what being in heaven meant?

◇ ◇ ◇

The plane lands in a very big airport. There are so many people that Sabine is frightened she will get lost. All around her people are talking to each other, and she can't understand a word that they say. Her head begins to ache. She is so cold that she has to jiggle about to keep warm.

"Is this the UK?" she asks Mama.

"Yes, this is the UK."

"Will *they* come after us?" says Sabine.

"No," says Mama. "We're too far away. We're safe now.."

Sabine feels a smile stretching over her face. She wants to dance with joy. She doesn't mind the cold if she is safe from *them*!

◇ ◇ ◇

More queuing. At last they reach the head of the queue. A tired looking *mzungu* says, "Papers please!"

"*Nous sommes des refugiés, moi et mes enfants,*" says Mama in a low voice. "My children and I are refugees!"

"Asylum-seekers?" says the *mzungu*. He looks at Mama's passport. "Democratic Republic of Congo? Do you speak any English?"

Mama shakes her head. "*Non. Seulement Français, Lingala, Kiswahili, et un peu de...* No, only French, Lingala, Kiswahili, and a little..."

"*Français?* French?" says the *mzungu*. He points at some chairs. "Wait over there! I'll get someone from Immigration to see you."

He gives the passport back to Mama.

◇ ◇ ◇

The *mzungu* from Immigration barks out his questions like an angry dog. He has an interpreter to help him to understand what Mama says, because he doesn't speak French. He writes down everything Mama says.

"Passport, please!"

"This is a false passport!" Mama says. "I have no papers. We had to leave in a hurry."

"What is your real name?"

"Celeste Nzuki."

"Why did you come here?"

"To get away from the war!"

The man scratches away on his piece of paper.

Sabine stops listening. She doesn't want to hear about the war. She starts playing with Didi's fingers. Suddenly a large tear plops on to Didi's hand.

"*They* shot my husband!" Mama says.

Baba has been shot? Is that why Baba isn't coming back? Sabine's head feels muddled and heavy. She doesn't know what to think.

"Is that all the luggage you've got?"

"Just this bag and a bundle of clothes."

"Where's the bundle?"

"They took it away!" Mama tells him. "They said they would give it back to us when we got here!"

"You were supposed to go and get it!" frowns the *mzungu*. "Go with the interpreter and she'll help you to find it. Then come back here!"

◇◇◇

They follow the interpreter to a large hall. Suitcases are travelling round and round on a machine. Every so often someone steps forward and takes one away.

"No sign of your bundle here!" says the interpreter. "Let's try another one!"

They trail round after the interpreter, searching one carousel after another, but there is no sign of a blue skin-wrapped bundle.

"Baa!" Lou's face is screwed up with worry.

"We'll report it lost!" says the interpreter. "Where's your ticket?"

"What ticket?" says Mama. "Oh! That sticker!" She searches in her bag, but she can't find it.

Lou bursts into frantic tears. "I want my Baa!"

"Nothing we can do about it without a ticket," sighs the interpreter. "We'd better go back to Immigration and tell them what's happened."

Sabine's chest feels tight. She knows that they won't see Baa again. She wants to scream and cry, but her screams have got lost inside her and her tears won't come out.

Lou has to be dragged screaming out of the hall.

❖ ❖ ❖

The interpreter tells the *mzungu* from Immigration what has happened. He nods, he doesn't look up. He is still scribbling on his forms.

He tells Mama to put her thumb on a black pad and press it down on his paper. Then the *mzungu* wipes his forehead with a paper handkerchief and asks Mama another question.

At last the *mzungu* says, "I am keeping your false passport because you are not entitled to use it. Here are your new papers. You can use them to prove that you are claiming asylum."

❖ ❖ ❖

They are taken to another room. Someone brings a bottle for Didi. Two plates are put on to the table. One is piled with yellowy-brown sticks, the other with white squares.

"What's that?" asks Thérèse.

"Sandwiches and chips!" smiles the welfare worker.

"I want *ugali*!" Lou says, sullenly. "And I want Baa!"

"They haven't got *ugali*," says Mama shortly.

The children pick at the food. It isn't what they are used to, and they don't eat very much.

At last the talking finishes. They are driven to a house and shown into a big room with lots of mattresses propped up on legs. There are other women and children there, some talking, some sleeping and some sitting and staring into space.

"I don't want to sleep on those!" cries Thérèse.

"You'll have to," says Mama. "That's how people sleep here. You can come in with Didi and me, and Lou can sleep with Sabine. Up you go!"

Sabine snuggles down with Lou. Sabine doesn't like the heaviness of the covers, or their strange, sickly sweet smell, but Lou smells like home. Sabine puts her arms round Lou and holds on tight. That way they won't fall off the mattress. She is almost asleep when Lou says tearfully, "I want Baa!"

Sabine jerks awake.

"Baa's not here," she says. She feels a dull ache

in her chest.

"Where is she?"

Sabine's throat goes tight. She doesn't know what to say. Then she has a sudden inspiration. "Baa's gone to live with the angels!"

"With the angels?" Lou says, doubtfully.

That's right! Baa's gone to see Baba. She's flying round and round the world in an aeroplane!"

"Is Baba on the aeroplane?"

"Yes!" says Sabine. "Angie's looking after them both. And when we go back home, maybe we'll see Baba and Baa on the aeroplane!"

"Yes!" responds Lou. "We'll see them on the aeroplane!"

She snuggles up to Sabine.

"Love you," she says, sleepily.

"Love you, too!" answers Sabine.

Lou goes to sleep, but Sabine lies awake, listening to the sleepy murmurs around her. Baba is lost. So is Baa. The UK is a horrible place. It is full up with *mzungus* and there isn't enough space. Why has Mama brought them here? Why couldn't they have stayed at home?

Only Up From Here
by Sulaiman Addonia

Kareem is sent away by his mother to flee the devastating war between his country, Eritrea, and Ethiopia. It is the end of the 1980s, a period which saw some of the most intense fighting in a war that lasted for over 30 years. This story is about a young East African boy in a big European city.

I remember what you told me when you put me on top of a camel to begin my journey from Eritrea to an unknown destination in the western world. You said, "Kareem, you will be in a safe haven. Safe from this haunting death. The Europeans are good people. They will look after you, send you to school, buy you clothes and food, until the day comes when you will look after yourself. In Europe, you will not hear the sound of bombs. Only the sound of music."

The morning of that day was beautiful. It was the time when everything was quiet. There was only silence and a blue sky, no Ethiopian bomber planes circling in the sky and no machine guns spreading bullets everywhere.

I woke up at 6am, washed my face, took a bucket and rode my donkey to get water from the river that was two hours away.

Alem was a beautiful donkey. She was as black as me, like roasted coffee beans. My face was long and thin just like Alem's, and my teeth stuck out like hers. She never threw me off her back and I never hit her or dug my heels into her. We were a perfect match.

On our way to the river, Alem was tossing up the stones with her hooves. I was enjoying the silence and the fresh air. I was just glad to have survived the night's bombardment.

Then I heard you calling me. "Kareem, stop. Stop."

Out of nowhere, a man appeared behind you. My first thought was that you were going to marry him. I would have understood. Since father died in the war with Ethiopia, you have found it difficult to look after me. You sold tea and coffee at your little stall in the market. But as you earned so little, I had to fetch water to sell to our neighbours.

"I need the donkey. You go back home," you said.

"But Mother, I must sell some water today," I said.

"Just listen to what I am asking you to do, son," you said.

You rode the donkey and went off with the man.

❖ ❖ ❖

You came back in the evening, when the sun disappeared leaving behind darkness, moon and stars. You didn't say a word. You just lit the oil lamp, took your prayer rug and started praying.

I watched you as you went on kneeling, and recited some verses from the Koran. You weren't your normal self. Usually you didn't pray at this time. Instead this was the time when you told me stories until I fell asleep. I was surprised. I wondered if you were thinking of leaving me and running away with that man I saw in the morning. I wanted to cry.

You almost wailed your prayer, "Please God, keep my son safe. Please grant him safety. I beg you, God."

I asked myself why you were so worried about me. Was something bad about to happen?

Then you stood up, moved towards me, and dragged me from my bed.

In complete silence you dressed me in my black trousers, a white T-shirt, and sandals. Then you dragged me out of our hut.

"Where are we going?" I asked you.

"The time has come," you said.

"Time for what?"

"To leave."

"Why are we leaving?"

"I am not leaving," you said. "You are leaving on your own."

"But Mum," I cried, "I don't want to leave without you." I screamed loudly so that our neighbours could hear and help me but nothing happened.

"You will be fine," you said as you led me towards the hills and the bushes.

I begged you again, "But I don't want to be without you, Mum."

You said nothing. Your silence hurt me more than the mosquito bites that were stinging my arms and face.

Then you spoke, "You will go to Europe. It is a safe place. The man you saw earlier this morning told me. He sent his son there and he is doing well."

"Where is Europe?"

"I don't know, but it is far from here."

"Mum, why don't you come with me?"

"I don't have money for both of us," you said. "I can't bear the thought of seeing you die like the others. I have seen what these bombs do to children. I won't cover your grave with mud. I'd rather see you leave me in one piece."

"But Mum, I am happy here with you. I'm not scared. How can you let me go?"

You were silent.

The smugglers were waiting for us. They were surrounded by oil lamps. I had never seen so many lamps. It was as if the stars had come down from the sky.

The men stood next to their camels, ready for the journey. You handed me to one of them. He said, "Allah is my witness that I will deliver your son to the businessman in Khartoum who will send him to a European country. He is good."

"I will miss you so much, my son," you said. You gave me one last hug and helped me get on the camel. "Promise me you will look after yourself."

"I will," I said.

"Promise you will always remember me?"

"I will," I said.

"And make sure you study hard and make me proud."

"I will."

The camel man suddenly shouted, "Woman, we don't have much time. The fighter planes will be coming, we must hurry."

I was in the saddle of the camel looking at your face. I saw you crying. I managed to touch your cheek.

Then the camels started to move. "Son?" you cried out as you ran behind the camel. "Son?"

◇ ◇ ◇

The camels crossed the border into Sudan safely. My guide helped me catch a bus to Khartoum. At the bus station, I met the man who would send me to Europe.

"I am Ali," he said, greeting me warmly.

For days he kept talking about his skills at faking passports and visas, and how he controls the gateway to the safe world of Europe. Then one day he said to me, "I have everything ready for you to go to London."

I didn't know where London was, but I arrived at its airport late one evening.

It took a few minutes for me to be transported by bus from the plane to immigration control with the rest of the passengers. I found myself joining a queue in front of a man sitting on a high chair behind a high table. He was checking passports. He looked stern. No smile, not a single expression on his face. I started shaking badly. I quietly recited verses from the Koran to calm me down. I prayed: "Please God, turn this man's heart into a gentle and caring heart like my mother's."

But somehow the worry kept mounting. I wanted to cry aloud and tell everyone that I didn't want to come here, that it was my mother who had sent me here, and that I have a fake passport, fake tourist visa, and fake age.

This reminded me to act how Ali told me to. "You must stand up tall and make yourself like an adult. If you don't, they will find out your real age and send you back. Behave like a man, just like it says in your new passport."

I stretched my neck, so that I looked taller;

narrowed my eyes; I tensed my jaw to give me a serious look; and I held my passport in my right hand with the elbow stretched out – just like the Ethiopian soldiers hold their guns.

Then it was my turn to give my passport to the man. He was checking it carefully, more than he did with the others. He took a long time. I wished you'd never sent me here. Bad thoughts about you entered my mind. For the first time in my life, I mumbled, "I hate my mother."

The man interrupted my thoughts and he spoke in English, which I didn't understand. I took my note and handed it to him. It was given to me by Ali. It said, *I don't speak English. I speak Tigrinya, the language of Eritrea. I am a tourist. I am staying in this hotel – 32–34 Bloomsbury Street, Bayswater.*

The man said something. I understood from the gesture of his hand – his index and thumb fingers rubbing each other slowly – that he was asking about how I would finance my stay. I handed him another note. It said, *I have £500 for two weeks stay.*

I was waved through.

'God,' I thought as I walked away from the immigration control, 'I am actually in London. I am safe.'

I stepped outside the lounge and searched for Ali's partner. He knew my flight schedule and was picking me up at the airport.

"It won't be difficult to recognise my partner," Ali had told me. "He is my brother and he looks like me."

At once I saw the man. He looked so much like Ali, I thought they must be twins.

"I am Mustafa," the man said, as soon as I approached him. "Everything is arranged. Tonight you will sleep at my place. Tomorrow I will take you to the Home Office and you will ask for asylum. OK?"

"OK."

◇ ◇ ◇

Even though it was quiet and safe, the first night in London was harder than sleeping in our hut under the noisy Ethiopian planes.

I started thinking of you. I couldn't sleep. How could I, knowing that a bomb could have finally found you? We had a saying in our village: "A time comes when even a blind man will hit his target."

I heard the sound of rain falling in the street. I opened the window and stared across the quiet street.

There were plenty of parked cars and trees on each side of the road. The autumn wind kept bringing leaves down to the ground. The street was like a Persian rug, painted by yellow, red and orange leaves. Then suddenly a cat appeared from under a parked car. It was meowing. And just like me, it was young, lost, and alone.

Then I missed you even more. I wanted to run to the Home Office and tell them to deport me. I wanted to be with you and my donkey, Alem. But then I remembered the promise I made to you. So I began to memorise the story that I was going to tell the Home Office people the next morning.

◇◇◇

"The most important thing to remember is to say your age," said Mustafa. "Tell them the age in the passport and not your real age. OK? Don't worry about the rest of the story. Just tell the truth. Your country is at war. That's enough for you to seek asylum."

At the Home Office, we joined a very long queue. There were all sorts of people queuing. We all stood holding our documents. I saw a lot of people concentrating hard and mumbling words. They were memorising the stories they were going to tell the Home Office people. I started to go over my story once again.

The queue was moving very slowly. It took almost half a day before it was my turn to face the man behind the window. I told him my story in Tigrinya and Mustafa translated. I was hesitating a lot. But Mustafa kept a straight face throughout my session. The Home Office man wrote my story down. I was given papers confirming that I was an asylum-seeker in this country. But I was told that I would have to wait for a decision.

I felt happy that I had not been harmed by the Home Office. But my happiness was cut short when Mustafa took me straight to a charity that gives houses and support to people like me and left me there.

"My job is done. This is not the government. So don't be scared. These people are very helpful," he said.

"Are we going to meet again?" I asked him. He was the only person I knew in this country.

"There are translators here who speak Tigrinya. An advisor will see you shortly. My job is finished," he said and he patted me on my afro-hair before leaving.

The advisor, who sat behind a desk, introduced herself as Diane. Her words were translated to me by the Eritrean man who sat beside her. His name was Eyob. Diane found me a room in a place called Mile End.

The room I was given was on the ground floor. The other four men in the house were in their late 30s and white. They were Eastern European refugees. They looked very upset when they saw me. So I locked my door and stayed there all day.

Days went by and I had no one to talk to. It was

as if I was in a jail and the four men were the guards. I couldn't watch TV because they were in the living room all day doing nothing but watching TV, eating and sometimes sleeping there too.

One evening they went out and I thought I'd have my dinner in the kitchen: cornflakes with milk. It was all I was eating day and night, until I taught myself how to cook. But as soon as I started eating, two of them came back and came straight to the kitchen.

They opened the fridge and started drinking alcohol. You had told me it was forbidden in our religion to drink or even touch alcohol. I hated its smell. One of them started shouting at me in his language. He had long hair and had drawings over his left arm, like henna drawings. But his drawing was not made of lines. It was a picture of a violent dragon.

He touched my hair with his right index finger. Both men started laughing. I decided to go to my room with my food. But one of them took my bowl and poured a bit of alcohol in it. I ran to my room and locked my door.

"How could this happen to me?" I asked myself. "Only three weeks ago, I was with my mother. There was war and I could have died, but I had my mother beside me. I had her love and care."

I cried myself to sleep.

◇◇◇

Next morning I woke up smiling. I'd had a beautiful dream.

I was running from the Ethiopian fighter planes. You suddenly appeared from nowhere and hugged me tightly. Then the fighter planes turned into butterflies with beautiful colours, and humming wings. Then you kissed me and told me that you were with me in spirit and that I should do what I promised you. Then I too turned into a butterfly. And as I flew away from you, you blew me kisses and told me we would meet again soon.

The dream made me feel good. "This time," I thought to myself, "I will make my journey on my own."

I packed my bag and headed to the charity organisation.

"Are you OK?" Eyob asked me.

"I want to tell you and Diane a secret," I said. "But can I trust her?"

"Diane has worked with refugees for over 30 years," he replied. "She even worked with Eritrean refugees living in refugee camps in Sudan. She took care of me when I came here 7 years ago. Without her help, I wouldn't be where I am today. So yes, you can trust her."

Then he added, "Kareem, what is it you want to tell Diane?"

"It is about my age," I said.

"What about your age?"

"I am..." Then I stopped.

"Kareem, did you change your age?"

I said nothing.

He added, "When I came to this country, I lied about my age too. My businessman thought that increasing my age would get me through the immigration control at the airport as I was travelling on my own. But if you tell the government you are an adult, they will think of you as one. They will put you in adult accommodation. You will go to college and not to school. If you tell us your real age, we will send you to a place where you will live and go to school with other children, where someone will teach you how to wash and cook."

I looked at Diane to see if she was as nice as he was saying. I searched her face, and it reminded me of yours. Her face was white, but both your faces had the same expression. She had a gentle face that had wrinkles of wisdom below the eyes. Her big eyes made me comfortable every time she looked at me. Her smile was just like yours: a smile that melted away your worries and made you feel happy.

"Trust me," she said, in broken Tigrinya.

I stared at her speechless. Eyob was laughing. "Yes, she knows a bit of Tigrinya too."

"I am not 17 like it says in my Home Office

paper. I am 14 years old next week," I said, and I started to cry uncontrollably.

◇ ◇ ◇

Now I am here in a house for unaccompanied asylum-seeking children. I feel better, although I still miss you deeply. Last night I talked to Diane about this. She said I could write you a letter – but I had a better idea. I decided to write you a letter each time I begin to fulfil one of the promises I made to you when I began my journey on the camel.

This morning I have started studying at a school. The whole class today was an English lesson. It is 9pm now, and I thought I would write and tell you that I am working hard and that when I finish my English course, I will go to secondary school, then to college and then to university. After that I will work and then bring you here with my money.

That is why it can only be up from here for me. So please keep safe and alive until that day.

Samir Hakkim's
Healthy Eating Diary
by Miriam Halahmy

How do you explain life in Baghdad to your classmates in an English primary school? It is 2002 and Samir's family have all been arrested by Saddam Hussein, so his uncle has smuggled him out of Iraq to save his life. All alone in England with no friends or family, ten-year-old Samir writes a diary to try and understand his new life.

Monday 8th July 2002
BREAKFAST : Rice Krispies, milk, Crunchie,
chewing gum
SCHOOL LUNCH : chicken nuggets, chips,
baked beans, chocolate sponge and custard
DINNER : Pot noodle

Miss Broome has asked us to write down everything we eat this week. That won't take long so I've decided to write my own diary at the back of the notebook, in my secret language – Arabic.

No one knows Arabic here. They can't even say my name properly. My name is Samir, the last bit is like the English word, *ear*. But they just say Sammy, or Sam or even Sambo and then everyone laughs.

I don't know why. Nissim would know. He used to laugh at me when I forgot the verses from the Koran. But he never ever let anyone else laugh at me. "That's what big brothers are for," he would say.

I haven't seen Nissim for nine months, three weeks and two days. They made him join the army. The soldiers came and dragged him out of the house and Mum was screaming so much I couldn't even say goodbye. Two months later Uncle Sayeed came to my room and shook me awake. He gave me a plastic carrier bag. "Put your things in here, Samir, and then you are leaving." It was the middle of the night and I was so sleepy I could hardly move. I packed my toothbrush but no underwear. I couldn't find my sweater or my shoes, so I left in my socks and a T-shirt and shorts. It wasn't very cold in Baghdad in January but when we arrived at Heathrow it was like standing in a giant air conditioning unit. England is always cold, especially here in Havant, near the sea.

A lady came with me to Heathrow. Uncle Sayeed said she was a friend and I had to be a very good boy. I slept all the way on the plane and when we arrived and got through the passport bit, she just disappeared. I was left standing there with my carrier bag, in my socks like a baby. Eventually some people came and took me to a children's home. I was so scared I stayed in bed for two days and every time someone came in the room I pretended I was asleep.

I liked the children's home. Steve and Wayne, the helpers, played football with us every day and there was another boy, Marwan, who's also ten. He was from Saudi so we spoke Arabic all the time. They gave us nice food too. We had English food like pizza and hamburgers and chips, but sometimes they made Arabic food; *tahini* with salad or rice and *foul medames*, which is a kind of big brown bean.

My mother made *foul* in big bowls, like the soup bowls in England, with lemon juice and chopped parsley and a hard boiled egg on the side. Sometimes I was in such a hurry to go out and play that I didn't eat it all and she'd say, "Don't waste food, Samir. In Iraq, we don't have enough good food." But I would just laugh and run out anyway. Now I would give anything for a bowl of my mother's *foul* and egg. But it's too late.

We learnt to speak English in the children's home and I learnt really quickly. My father always said I was good at languages. He was teaching me French and I was always top in Arabic in my school in Baghdad. I'm the bottom in most things now and there's no one to help me with my homework, like Dad did. At least I'll do French when I go up to the High School in September.

If I'm still here.

I'm not planning on staying, trust me. All I want

is to go home to Baghdad and find my mother and Nissim and Uncle Sayeed. Then we can go and rescue my father from prison. Nissim said he was dead. He screamed it at me the day before the soldiers came and took him away. But I don't believe him.

After three months in the children's home they said I had to go into a foster home and Marwan couldn't come with me. I didn't want to go, but they said I had to. The government wanted all refugees like me and Marwan spread around the country, like jam on bread, so that there were not too many of us in one place. "Then there won't be any trouble," said Wayne. I'm not any trouble, neither is Marwan. But no one listens to refugees, especially not children. I ended up living with Aunty Jones and the twins who are only two, in a place in England where no one knows any Arabic at all.

Tuesday 9th July 2002
BREAKFAST : bread and jam, coke,
packet of cheese and onion crisps
SCHOOL LUNCH : turkey twizzlers, chips,
blancmange and chocolate sauce
DINNER : egg and chips

I've been with Aunty Jones for three months now and she's never heard of *foul medames*. I looked in Somerfield, but I couldn't see any there either.

"You're an English boy now, Sammy," said Aunty Jones. "You eat English food and speak English. Look, I got you a Manchester City baseball cap in the market."

But when I wore it to school, all the kids laughed at me.

"What a bunch of muppets," said Mikey Fern. "Looks good on you, Samir, man."

Mikey is the only person who bothers to say my name properly. He's my best friend; well to be honest, he's my only friend. I've been teaching him Arabic, like *shukran* (thank you) and *inshallah* (God willing). The other kids get really mad when we speak our secret language.

Today Miss Broome took us to the library to do some research on our history topic, Britain between the Wars. We had to walk in pairs through the town and some of the parents came to supervise. Melanie Richard's mum, was walking near me and Mikey, and suddenly we saw an old lady sitting on the pavement, throwing bits of bread to some pigeons. Melanie's mum said in a really disgusted voice, "How dirty! Those birds are just vermin."

Mikey was pulling my arm because I was standing still, staring at the pigeons. "Come *on*, Samir, what's the matter with you?" Mikey said, but I didn't move. My father used to keep pigeons on the roof of our house in Baghdad. I helped him make the cages for them and every day we would train them to fly and then return to our calls. Everyone kept pigeons in Baghdad and you could hear all the different calls round the roof tops in the evenings after the men came home from work. In the summer, when it was hot, we slept out on the roof. Nissim and I would lie awake half the night, counting stars and in the morning the first thing we heard was the beautiful sound of the pigeons cooing.

Mikey was pulling my arm and I knew I had to go, but I just wanted to sit down on the pavement and cry, like a little kid. I miss my mum and dad and I want someone from home to put their arms around me and tell me everything is going to be ok. But there's just Mikey and Aunty Jones, who doesn't think about anything except winning the lottery and the twins, who can't even talk properly.

At least there's Mikey.

Wednesday 10th July 2002
BREAKFAST : nothing, I overslept
and had to run to school
SCHOOL LUNCH : sausages, baked beans, mash,
vanilla ice-cream and sprinkles
DINNER : shepherd's pie, peas, broad beans
(they are just like foul, only green) salad,
home-made trifle or strawberries and cream
(I had both)

Best day for ages. Mikey invited me home to his house for tea and to play on his Play Station. His mum and dad are so nice. They smiled at me all the time and told me to eat as much as I liked. *Wicked*. (I had to write 'wicked' in English, we don't have it in Arabic. It means really, really good.) They couldn't quite get my name right, but when they called me Sammy it sounded ok, at least they tried.

Mikey's big brother Darren was there too. He's fourteen, one year younger than Nissim and he couldn't believe it when I said Nissim was in the army. I said that Nissim wanted to be an engineer. "Don't they have universities in Iraq?" asked Darren. And I didn't know what to say. Mikey's dad works in a bank and his mum is a nurse.

How could I tell them my dad was a captain in the Baghdad Police?

How could I tell them how everything went wrong and how no one would tell me what happened? "You're too young, Samir," Uncle Sayeed said. Mum just cried and cried and Nissim banged his fists on the table. I've never been so scared, not even when I was left alone at Heathrow airport in my socks.

One day, instead of Dad putting the real criminals in prison, Saddam Hussein put *him* in prison. For weeks we tried to find out what had happened, but when they took Nissim into the army we stopped trying. Uncle Sayeed said it wasn't safe.

Then they came and took Mum away while I was at school. That night Uncle Sayeed sent me to England.

But I can't tell Mikey's family all this. They might think I was the son of a criminal and then they won't let me and Mikey play together any more and I'll be all alone again.

What do they know about life in Iraq and how people disappear all the time?

So I just said nothing and Mikey said, "Can we go now, Mum?" and his mum smiled and said we could and that was that.

I hope Mikey invites me again.

Thursday 11th July 2002
BREAKFAST : Rice Krispies, no milk (it was off),
tea without milk or sugar (we were out of sugar)
SCHOOL LUNCH : chips (I didn't feel like
anything else, sorry Miss)
DINNER : cheese sandwich, crisps, coke

I didn't feel like eating anything today. Mikey tried to cheer me up at lunch but I just wanted to be on my own. I hate this country. I hate the English, they don't understand anything. If Nissim was here he'd beat them all up. Punch their lights out, as Melanie Richard's cousin says, every time I pass the ball to someone else. "Stupid Paki, pass it to me or I'll kill ya," he yells at me. His gang are real racists.

They don't even know where Baghdad is.

But I don't care about them, not while Mikey's my friend. It's the adults who are the really stupid ones.

We had a lady come into our class today to tell us about the Second World War. She said she was a refugee when she was a little girl. That made me sit up and listen. Mikey looked across at me. I've told him a bit about how I got here, so I gave him the thumbs up and grinned. She told us how she came to England all alone on a train, when she was ten years old, the same age as me.

"I came from Germany," said the lady. She had a funny accent too. "My family was Jewish and the Nazis didn't like the Jews. So my parents sent me to England. I never saw anyone from my family again. They were all gassed in the camps."

It was like someone had exploded a bomb inside my head. My hand shot up. I had to shout out, even if the whole class laughed. They had to listen to me this time.

"Yes, Sammy," said Miss Broome. She is always kind to me, even if she doesn't say my name properly. "Do you want to ask Eva a question?"

"It's just like me, Miss," and Miss Broome nodded encouragingly. Maybe they did want to hear my story, but even more important I had to tell them about Aunty Selma. "My aunty was gassed too, Miss, and..."

But they stopped me right there, just like Saddam Hussein. You have to be really careful what you say in Baghdad or they take you away. And it was just like that in class.

"Sammy, what are you saying!" said Miss Broome in a shocked voice and the lady from the train was shaking her head and looking angry. I suddenly felt very scared as though I had done something really wrong and then I muttered I needed to go to the toilet. Miss Broome nodded and I just slunk out of the classroom. Melanie Richards and her cousin sniggered as I went passed them.

My Aunty Selma is a Kurd from a place called Halabjah in northern Iraq. Saddam Hussein didn't like the Kurds so he dropped gas bombs on them and gassed all the people, just like the Germans did to the Jews in the war.

Aunty Selma was ten and she was visiting a friend in another village. But all her family were killed. She was sent to live with her grandparents in Baghdad and when she grew up she married Uncle Sayeed. But she still cries about her family.

Mikey wanted to know why I wouldn't play with him today. He said I should talk to Darren. "He's always watching the news and reading books, Samir. He would know about the Kurds and the gas."

But I just shook my head and walked away.

Friday 12th July 2002
BREAKFAST : nothing
SCHOOL LUNCH : nothing
DINNER : chicken casserole, mash,
broad beans (loads), carrots,
apple pie and custard.

I ran away from Aunty Jones this morning and didn't go to school. Mikey found me in the park and took me to his house. His mum said I could stay the night and she rang Aunty Jones and got her to agree. She just said I was a bit homesick and sleeping over with Mikey would take my mind off things and it was the weekend. Mikey's mum said she would come into school on Monday morning and speak to Miss Broome so I wouldn't get into trouble.

Aunty Jones was angry with me for not going to the shop for her this morning. She wanted some tea bags and she said she couldn't leave the twins. When I said, "No, I'm too sleepy," she started yelling at me, saying I was too much trouble and made a lot of mess around the place, which isn't true, and moaned about the food all the time, which is a little bit true.

Darren was brilliant. "She's just a stupid..." he yelled but his mum cut him off. Then Darren started again, "Well, whatever, she doesn't treat our Sammy properly," and Mikey said, "*Samir!*" and

Darren said, "Yeah, well, Sam – *ear*" and I couldn't help grinning because he called me 'our Sammy' as if I belonged to his family. It felt so good I wanted to leap up and punch the air like football strikers on the telly.

But Darren hadn't finished. "Samir has come to England because he needs a safe place to live and he doesn't know what has happened to his family, and look who he gets landed with."

"She doesn't even give him proper food," said Mikey quietly and Mikey's mum said, "Is that true Sammy, love?" and I just shrugged. Nothing's going to change. Not until Mum and Dad and Nissim get here and rescue me.

Anyhow, one good thing. Darren said it was nearly the summer holidays and he was going to get me and Mikey a job selling ice-cream on the beach. He's got a friend who'll let us do it, even though we're only kids. And I thought, I could save my money up for when everyone comes over and then maybe we could get a little house together. *Wicked*!

Monday 15th July 2002
Sorry miss, I didn't have time to do Saturday
and I didn't eat much on Sunday.
Didn't feel very hungry. I pinched an apple from
the fruit bowl, so that's healthy, isn't it?

I haven't written in this diary since Friday night and

so much has happened. But it seems even more important now to write it all down. Darren says we should keep records so that we know what goes on in the world, so this is my record.

For Nissim and for Mum and Dad and for Uncle Sayeed and Aunty Selma.

I had a brilliant day on Saturday. First of all Mikey's mum cooked us a huge breakfast, with eggs and little fried potatoes and baked beans. When we couldn't eat any more, Darren, Mikey and me went to the beach. My jeans were soaked to the knees but it was a sunny day. It reminded me of holidays by the sea at Basra, swimming with Dad and Nissim.

Then we went and had ice-creams and Darren introduced us to his mate, Jonno, and Jonno said 'course we could come and help him on the beach at the end of term. We would get twenty pence for every ice-cream we sold and Mikey reckoned we could make ten pounds each day. Darren laughed and said, "Yeah right. Only if the weather's good, mate."

Mikey's mum made us the best lunch yet: roast chicken and roast potatoes and Yorkshire pudding, with peas, carrots and of course, my absolute favourite – broad beans, great big fat ones. "Bought them especially for you, Sammy," she said with a big smile. More ice-cream for pudding and then we went out again. There was a big market and a fair with rides, right down the main street. Darren paid for me and Mikey to go on the dodgems and we all crashed into each other like maniacs. It was amazing!

The market was great. All the stalls were piled high with fruit and vegetables. "I used to go to the market in Baghdad and carry the bags for my mum," I said to Mikey, and Darren looked really interested. "What food did they have?" he asked. "Watermelon and cheese and barrels of olives and loads and loads of beans," I grinned.

But I wasn't grinning inside. I was aching for home, for the Shorja market, three streets from my house. I used to grumble when Mum made me carry home the big green watermelons and I wanted to go and play football with my friends. Once I shouted at her, "You're not an old woman, you carry it, I'm going out!"

I'd give anything to go back and carry that watermelon home. Mum's face would break into her best smile, the one she keeps for me and Nissim.

When we got back to Mikey's house, laughing because the girl on the coconut shy had asked Darren out and he didn't know what to say, the front door was wide open. "Someone's here," said Darren and went in first.

Aunty Jones was standing in the corridor with the twins rolling at her feet. She was saying something to Mikey's mum but they stopped talking when they saw me. "You've got to come home now,

Sam, love," said Aunty Jones. She was trying to impress Mikey's mum with how fond she was of me. But I could tell Mikey's mum wasn't taken in, what with the cigarette in Aunty Jones' mouth and the twins with their smeary faces.

"You've had a phone call from a relative of yours, she's coming round tomorrow. Got to get your room ready. She'll have to sleep in there with you."

All the way home the twins whined for sweets and ice-cream, but all I could think was MUM! Mum was alive and she'd come to England to find me.

I asked Aunty Jones every question under the sun, but she couldn't tell me any more. Just that it was a woman, and she was coming down from London on the coach on Sunday.

Aunty Jones gave me an inflatable airbed to put on the floor and a couple of blankets. But she said she didn't have spare pillows. I cleared out all the drawers in the cabinet and stuffed my clothes under my bed. Mum would need loads more room than me. She had some really beautiful clothes at home.

Long after midnight I was still awake and I pulled open the curtains to try and see the stars, like we used to in Baghdad. But it was a cloudy night and I couldn't even see the moon.

Eventually, at around four, a taxi drew up outside and I ran out to see the back of a woman stooping through the front window to pay, her head wrapped in a black scarf. My heart was pounding in my chest and I couldn't breathe as the woman turned slowly round and then I saw who it was... Aunty Selma!

I just stood there like a statue. I couldn't move. But when Aunty Selma saw me she ran over and put her arms around me and started crying, just like she used to in Baghdad. Then the twins ran out into the street and flung their arms round my legs and they were howling and screaming. People going past must have thought we were a right bunch of idiots. So I picked up Aunty Selma's bags with the twins still gripping my legs, and managed to get everyone back through the front door and into the living room.

Aunty Selma and I talked half the night, and it was so good to talk Arabic after months of English all the time. Aunty Selma told me that she isn't sure where Mum and Dad are but she knows Nissim is alive! *Brilliant*! *Wicked*! He ran away from the army, a neighbour told her. Uncle Sayeed is going to stay in Baghdad and try to find my parents. Aunty Selma brought me a photo of Mum and Dad and me and Nissim, sitting in our garden in Baghdad, eating red watermelon. It made me so sad, I cried and Aunty Selma cried and put her arms around me until we fell asleep.

But when I woke up on Monday morning

I knew exactly what I had to do now.

Work hard, earn money selling ice-cream this summer and save and save. Because Nissim will get to England, I know he will. And when he does I want him to find me, his brother, Samir Hakkim, ready to help him.

For that I'm going to need money, buckets of it!

A Nice Quiet Girl
by Gaye Hicyilmaz

Kurds have fled Turkey and sought asylum in other lands over many years and for many reasons. The huge dam-building projects which displace communities and drown homes and historic sites in south-eastern Turkey are one of many causes of the bitter conflicts in this area. I've been a stranger in many places and met both the welcoming and unwelcoming heart. But this time, I thought I'd look within. This is a story from my childhood, when I was the one who looked the other way.

"*Tulip?*" snorted my older brother. "How could anyone call their daughter *Tulip?* Her parents should be shot for that, even if they are refugees. What a stupid name."

Dad chewed his steak. Mum shifted mushrooms around her plate.

"It isn't her real name," she said, "and you shouldn't joke about it."

My brother and I rolled our eyes. He's James and I'm Charlotte and as Jamie and Charlie, we didn't have name worries, thank goodness.

"So what *is* her real name?" I asked.

"Something Turkish or Kurdish," Mum said, "and impossible. That's why she's called 'Tulip' over here. And tomorrow…"

"Tomorrow's Saturday!" I reminded Mum.

"I know. And Tulip's coming tomorrow."

"She can't."

"Well, she is." Mum captured a mushroom. "Tulip's coming tomorrow because her mum's doing extra cleaning. Anyway, I'm sure she'll be lots of fun."

But Tulip wasn't fun and my mum must have known that, because after supper I learnt that Tulip had already been to our house a couple of times. Mum knew her. She'd come with her mother, Mrs Karahasan, who's been cleaning for us for weeks.

"Actually," Dad said, "she was here today. But you'd never have known. She's such a nice, quiet girl. She spent all morning in your room, Charlie, and I never heard a squeak."

I was speechless. I ran upstairs and suddenly noticed that a stranger had been in my room. Someone had touched my seaside collection: they'd moved the starfish nearer to the bits of coloured glass. I told Mum but she only shrugged.

"So?" she remarked. "I said she could look at your things."

"I bet she played my music!"

"Possibly." Dad looked up. "But if she did, she didn't disturb me. And that's not always the case with music from your room, is it, Charlie?"

I blushed. Sometimes his dental nurse had come

up to tell me to turn the volume down. At once!

"But..."

"Charlie!" Mum put her head on one side. "Tulip won't have done any damage. She's like her mum. Mrs K is so careful and so hard working. She cleans this house as if it was her own."

Dad nodded. And they were right, in a way: we'd never been so clean. Since Mrs K's arrival our house had sparkled, even though it was big and old and full of London dirt. I'd noticed the improvement as soon as I'd come in from school: the smooth, vacuumed floors, the hung-up jackets and the smell of lavender furniture polish.

But they were wrong about the damage and it wasn't just my star fish. When I tried to sleep that night, I couldn't get comfortable. I could feel exactly where somebody had lounged on my bed and changed my mattress to her shape. I'd tossed and turned. This was Tulip's fault. She was a fat lump, like her mother, and she'd dented my bed.

On Saturday morning, I overslept, then woke with a horrible start. Was that them, already? I rushed for the shower. I imagined this girl barging in and sprawling on the end of my bed. I'd be trapped under the duvet, getting hotter and sweatier and unable to get to the loo or inspect my spots.

Luckily, the bell wasn't Tulip and her mum: it was a patient for Dad. I showered for ages, then opened the window and watched the steam stream out. That's when I first saw her, at the far end of our street. I knew it was them. Mrs Karahasan is impossible to miss. She's vast and she always wears the same clothes: a bright green cardigan over a long, flowered skirt, with a green wool blanket thing over her head and shoulders. And there she was: this mountain of old clothes, striding up our street, with this *child* in tow.

Was *that* Tulip? I shivered and grabbed a towel to cover up.

They were holding hands! I couldn't believe it. I hadn't held hands for years. An arm, if I couldn't avoid it, but not a hand. Not flesh.

Tulip was wearing socks: white, lacy knee socks under a hideous brown checked skirt with a quilted purple jacket on top. Gleaming chestnut hair streamed down her back. Someone had tied a soppy white bow amongst it, as though she was some old person's pet. In the mirror my reflection had steamed up.

In two seconds I'd dressed in my oldest, dirtiest black jeans and one of Jamie's torn T-shirts. I left my hair sopping wet and sticking out.

"Morning Mrs K!" I called cheerily over the banisters. "Couldn't Tulip come after all?"

If she replied, I didn't hear because the practice door opened down in the hall and the noise of dental drills and patients smothered her quiet, foreign voice. I hesitated. Then I heard a tread. Was this interloper coming up, uninvited? I tore down both flights. I couldn't let her ambush me at the top. I intended to just miss crashing into her, but it didn't work. She stepped aside. I almost tripped.

"Hi! I'm Charlie. It's *so* nice of you to come!"

"Hello." She wasn't fat. Or skinny, like me. Her eyes were as softly green as two spring leaves in shade. Now she wore a pink cardigan with flowers embroidered at its neck. She was older than me, perhaps, with what Gran calls a 'bust'. She bent down and straightened both socks. Her shoes were new and cheap.

"Wow!" I perched on the edge of a stair and inspected her. Kindly.

"So, what would *you* like to do, Tulip?"

"What you like to do." She'd whispered. I wasn't sure she'd understood.

"Me? Nothing! But this is *your* day. We'll do what *you* want to do." I shook my head vigorously and several drops spotted the perfect leather. She'd stood two stairs below me staring at her shoes. Her skin was smooth, her lashes long and dark. She was doll-like, as though she too had been lifted from a box.

"How about music?" I suggested. "Shall we listen to some CDs?"

"Yes. Listen to… music."

I'd sat at my computer. She'd remained standing

in the middle of the carpet, just as if she'd never been in my room before and never lolled on my bed. We listened in total silence. She traced the checks on her skirt with a finger. The nail was quite bitten off. When I couldn't stand it any longer, I jumped up.

When I listened to music with my best friend Emma, we did dance routines and said stuff that we'd never have said otherwise. Now I had to escape.

"Shall we go in the garden?" I asked.

"You go in garden?" she asked back.

"*We* can," I replied patiently. "I mean, *I* can go into my garden any time. But you're the guest. We'll do what *you* want. You've only got to say."

"We... I say... I like garden..."

"Whatever."

We had a long, narrow back garden. It wasn't anything special but it was nice enough, with old walls and flowers and things in the borders down the sides. Dad likes a lawn but he'd never minded when we'd played on it. Two years before, when Emma and I were eleven, we'd built a bike slalom and scuffed his grass a lot.

That Saturday, Tulip stood on the edge. I watched the dew darken the spotless leather of her shoes. Upstairs, duvets tumbled from the bedroom windows and hung there in the mild autumn sun.

We played badminton first. Tulip was hopeless. I don't think she returned a single shot.

She watched the shuttlecock pinging through the air, then ran and picked it up. I won every game. I couldn't lose. I beat her at mini golf and afterwards at darts. Then, searching for something easier still, I drew out hopscotch on the patio, between the tubs.

I hadn't played hopscotch for years and I enjoyed it like a kid. And beat her. She couldn't even hop. Finally, I spent ages setting up the slalom and then discovered that she couldn't ride a bike. So I had all the goes while she did time keeping, or pretended to.

It rained after lunch. We played Scrabble and I put 'onyx' on a treble and got the best score of my life. She wrote 'dog' and 'red' and wasted her 's' in 'is'. During our third game Mum returned loaded with supermarket bags. She pointed out that it was after five: the Karahasans should have left at three, to catch their bus. She gave Mrs K an extra £5, in case they had to take a cab.

After Tulip had gone I was fed up. I put my head round the surgery door, which I'm not supposed to do. Luckily, the last patient had gone. Dad was tidying up.

"Had a good time?" he asked through his paper mask.

"Bearable."

"She seems like a nice girl," he took off his goggles, "with the patience of a saint."

"What do you mean?"

"Come on, Charlie. My surgery does overlook the garden."

"So?"

"So, nothing. And," he smiled, "she's got the most beautiful teeth."

"What? Is she a patient of yours?"

"Hardly!" He laughed. "Not with teeth like that. I haven't seen a set like that in years. She's lucky, with teeth *and* looks. Now, give me five minutes, then I'll give you a game of badminton that'll stretch you!"

"In the *rain*?" I snarled.

"Ah," he frowned. "Maybe not."

In the kitchen Mum was still unpacking bags.

"How was it?" she asked.

"Not bad."

"There you are." She tore open the jaffas and pushed them across.

"Will she come next Saturday?" I licked the chocolate top.

"'Fraid so. I need Mrs K to clean and Tulip can't be left alone, it seems. Can you bear it?"

"If I must."

"Charlie, you're a star! To spend your Saturday helping someone like that."

I shrugged.

"Mum? Why can't she stay alone?"

"Some sort of trouble with the dad." Mum

pulled a face and took another biscuit from the pack.

That night I cleaned my teeth until my gums bled.

The following Saturday I beat Tulip at Monopoly and Picka Sticks and Twister. I even beat her at a baby's game I'd found at the back of a cupboard, which involved jumping plastic frogs. Then I beat her at snap. We played more Monopoly in the afternoon and I thrashed her. I wiped her out, which is what Jamie always did to me, except he cheats.

But I didn't cheat. I didn't have to. Tulip couldn't get anything right. Luckily, she wasn't like me. She didn't mind being beaten, or not that much.

When I didn't see her for several weeks because Mum didn't need any Saturday cleaning, I missed her a lot. Then it was half-term so I asked Emma to stay for the week. My family never did anything exciting. Mum and Dad worked and I got fed up so I was glad when Emma said yes. I liked Emma, even though she was hard work. Her parents were finally divorcing, but they'd been fighting each other since we were in playgroup. I did get sick of hearing about their war. Now they were each buying new homes. Emma kept on about her two bedrooms: the new bunk beds that her mum said were perfect for sleep-overs in her flat, and the expensive music system that her father was installing just for her in his flat. It was a bit much.

Last time she'd stayed, we'd quarrelled, but in the end we'd made up.

On Saturday evening Mum announced that Tulip would be coming with Mrs K over half-term.

"What about Emma?" I'd gulped.

"What about her?"

I couldn't explain. How could I talk about decorating two bedrooms when I knew Tulip didn't even have one because she and her parents shared a single room in the hostel in town? And how could we go shopping, in Oxford Street, with a girl in white knee socks?

"Of course you can still go," Mum said. "It'll be an experience for Tulip. And you know what they say: safety in numbers. I'll certainly be happier if you're with Tulip. She's such a mature girl for her age."

"Mature?" I snorted. "She can't even hop! Still, no one's going to abduct us with her around."

"Why not?" Jamie looked up.

"Because," I groaned, "she's as thick as a plank."

"Rubbish," he grinned. "There's nothing plank-like about that girl. She's gorgeous."

He rippled his hands in the air. I felt sick.

"Jamie!" Mum was furious.

"OK." He blushed. "I shouldn't have. I just meant…"

"Don't worry," Mum patted my arm. "Ignore him."

"I'm not worried," I snapped. "I couldn't care less."

That night I shut myself in the bathroom and pulled at the skin on my bony chest to try and give myself breasts.

Emma's mum phoned late Sunday evening. She was so sorry. Emma couldn't come. It was her father's fault... My mum was holding the phone away from her ear. She was nodding: yes, yes, of course Charlie would understand. No, no, it wouldn't spoil any plans. Actually, Charlie had a visitor. No, no one from school. From abroad, the Middle East, actually, the daughter of someone we knew.

Tears threatened, but I held them back.

And it was terrific with Tulip. We got on brilliantly and I never got bored. We played loads of games and watched videos in between. On Wednesday we made Christmas cards, even though it was only October. I used to be very creative. I always had loads of ideas even though I couldn't be bothered to try them out. That afternoon, with Tulip watching, I did try and all my ideas worked out. I even gave her tips and let her copy my stuff.

When I made Christmas tree cards with the fold at the top, so that they stood up, she'd snipped through her folds. She stared open-mouthed as the useless halves flopped on to the table. I remember her glancing at me, guiltily, before she picked them up. If I'd been closer at that moment, I'm sure I'd have seen that her teeth weren't really as good as all that.

Emma phoned on Wednesday evening. She'd returned early. Could she come round? Now?

"No! I'm *so* sorry," I lowered my voice. "It's this girl, this daughter of somebody Mum knows. I've got to look after her all week. It's such a drag. She mustn't go out..."

"We'll stay in then."

"No! Nobody's supposed to know she's here."

"Why?"

"She's an asylum-seeker: one of those people who aren't supposed to be here, I think. That's why she mustn't go out."

"So? I won't tell."

"I know. But I can't take the risk."

"Fine!" She'd slammed down the phone.

It wasn't fine. I felt dreadful. I'd never lied before, or not like that. I'd lied about myself, obviously, when I'd needed to. For example, I'd lied to Mr Jenkins that I'd given in my maths project, when I hadn't, and he'd believed me and apologised for losing it, but I'd never lied like this. I'd never lied about somebody else's life. Never just made stuff up.

I shivered as I'd climbed into bed. But I'd lied for the right reasons. Hadn't I? I'd lied so that no one would get hurt.

Thursday was cold and bright. Tulip and I played Frisbee. I laughed so much Dad opened the surgery window and told me to shut up. Then he lowered his voice and told me that I wasn't being fair. I was furious. It wasn't my fault she couldn't catch.

On Friday, unexpectedly, Mum took me shopping. Tulip didn't come because we left early, to miss the morning rush.

As Christmas approached and there was more to do in the house, Tulip and her mum came most Saturdays and I looked forward to it all week. She wasn't a friend, exactly, but she was easy to be with. This was her second Christmas in London, but she didn't seem to know what Christmas was about. When I gave her a present, on Christmas Eve, she didn't give one back.

She didn't come much that spring. I saw her in the street a couple of times, in the yellow and brown uniform of Upton Comprehensive, but I didn't go over. I was with Emma both times and I was afraid that Emma might mention the asylum thing, so I looked the other way.

In May, Mum began her annual holiday brochure collection. She piled them by her chair and read out bits about water temperatures and food specialities and discounts. I never understood why she did this. We always went to Brighton for our holidays. We went every single year. It's where Dad grew up. His old family house, in a little crooked street just off the sea-front, was our holiday home. I liked it a lot. Jamie slept in Dad's old bedroom, with Dad's dusty model planes still dangling above his head. I slept in the tiny attic which Dad had converted. I planned a notice for the door that would read: 'Charlie's nest.'

One evening, while Mum was reading out a brochure entry about fried octopus in Turkey, Dad jumped up.

"Book your dream holiday in Turkey!" he'd shouted. "Eat fried octopus until you grow tentacles, I don't mind. But don't book a place for me. I shan't come."

"Darling!" Mum frowned. "You know perfectly well that I don't want to go to Turkey. It's probably not that nice. But it does say here that the food's delicious and that you're waited on hand and foot."

"Great. Book it. For yourself."

"No. I'm only *interested*. Especially after talking to Mrs K about Turkey. Can't I be interested in her world?"

I left. I wasn't interested in a Brighton versus Turkey match, or whatever game it was they wanted to play.

A few days later, Dad put down his breakfast mug in a very definite way.

"Well?" He cleared his throat and looked at Mum. "Hadn't we better tell her?"

My heart stopped. It fell through my chest. This was exactly the way Emma's parents had told her about their divorce. The juice extractor had been on, so she hadn't been sure what she'd heard, but hadn't liked to ask them to repeat it.

"Tell me what?" I made my voice calm but my thoughts raced ahead. I didn't want two bedrooms. I wanted...

"Your dad and I having been making holiday plans, and since you and Tulip get on so well, and since Jamie won't be coming this year, we thought you could ask her to come too. What do you think?"

"To Turkey? Yes!"

"Charlie," Dad frowned. "Don't be so stupid. The Karahasans are asylum-seekers. That's why they're here. They had to leave Turkey, apparently. They say they can't go back."

"No one's talking about Turkey," Mum was irritated. "We're going to Brighton, of course. And this is for you, Charlie, so that you won't be lonely, with Jamie in Spain with his mates. It'll be fun. You can show Tulip the sights."

"Won't she be homesick?" Suddenly, strangely, I remembered the way she and her mum always held hands. "Do you think she'll come all by herself?"

"She won't be by herself. Mrs K is coming with us, this year." Dad glanced at Mum. "So that we can taste delicious food and be waited on, hand and foot."

"Sugar!" I jumped up. "I've forgotten early tennis practice. I must dash."

I fled the house with my teeth uncleaned and my school bag unchecked. I was an hour early. The school gates were locked. I wandered back.

I saw Tulip and her mum turn out of a side street, a little way ahead. I ducked down behind a parked bus. They were walking, hand in hand, down the empty pavement towards Upton Comprehensive. Mrs Karahasan kept looking round. I watched. Did Tulip's mum walk her to school every morning and then come on up to us? For the first time I wondered about the hostel where they lived.

Then a van stopped. A man jumped out. He left the door open and ran straight across. Brakes screeched. Horns blared. The early morning traffic clogged up.

Someone cried out. When I dared look the man had hold of Tulip's wrist. He was swearing and yelling. Mrs K was keeping him off. On the other side of the street, a crowd gathered to watch. On my side people gave them a wide berth. If I'd been Tulip, I'd have pulled free and run. But she didn't. She stood as still as stone and let her mum drive that man off. He'd stumbled over the edge of the pavement and lurched back into the road.

Then, he'd slammed the van door shut and finally drove off.

I rested my cheek against the cold red bus.

"You all right, luv?" the bus driver asked through his window. I nodded and walked up the street. When I glanced back, Tulip was standing alone in the playground, straightening her socks.

It couldn't have lasted more than two minutes but I couldn't stop thinking about it. I did so badly in the French test that Miss Heston asked what was up. I wanted to tell, but couldn't and cried instead. I wanted to tell Emma, but didn't because she'd have launched into 'famous fights my parents have had'. Back home I nearly told Dad, but he'd have asked why I wasn't at early tennis, like I'd said. I didn't tell Mum either, in case she gave Mrs K the sack. That would have ruined everyone's holiday and I couldn't take the risk.

I decided that if the Brighton holiday went well, there was no point in saying anything. If it went badly, I would blame it on Tulip and her mum. I'd tell my parents what I'd seen and then they'd know that the Karahasans were rotten through and through.

Keeping quiet was the best solution. It worked, as well. Except that I dreamt about Tulip and the man and woke up crying in the night.

Mum's holiday planning was complicated. She would drive Mrs K down on Friday morning to 'open up the house'. Jamie said that it sounded like surgery. I thought of graves. Dad and I were to come on Sunday.

"What about Tulip?" I asked.

"She'll come with us," Dad said.

"She can't."

"Why not?"

"She can't stay by herself!"

"She won't be by herself. She'll be in a hostel full of people."

I swallowed down the thing that blocked my throat.

"Can't she stay here?" I asked.

"No."

"Please?" I turned to Mum. "You said she was *my* guest."

"For heaven's sake, Charlie, you're too old for this!" Dad was cross.

"But you said she was such a nice, quiet girl. A saint."

"Possibly, but I don't want her here. Two weeks with that pair is more than enough."

"But..."

"Charlie," Mum gave me a look. "Don't you think you're a bit obsessed with Tulip?"

I blushed. It wasn't true. It was just...

In the end Brighton was wonderful. It was the best holiday I'd ever had and the first time that I'd understood why Dad liked Brighton so much.

The days swept by like the tides on the beach. The sun shone and there wasn't a cloud, even at night. If I woke and craned out of my attic window, I always glimpsed a patch of distant glistening sea with the moon bright and unshadowed above.

Tulip, in a flowery pink skirt and plastic sandals, was happy to do whatever I suggested. We were all out of the house from morning till evening. Mum and Dad looked for jewellery and antiques in the little shops in the Lanes or went for walks up on the Downs. Tulip and I did beachy things. I'd never felt so grown-up. I ate non-stop and felt the beginnings of my bust. I bought us soft ices and chips and sugar dummies and burgers and warm candy floss. We licked and loitered and stared and munched. We wandered up and down the promenade and out along the pier. We looked at rude postcards and joke sunglasses and the hippies drumming on the beach. It was stuff I'd never have done on my own.

Each evening, when we all returned, Mrs K served a wonderful supper dish.

"See?" Mum teased Dad. "I told you Turkish food was good."

"Not Turkish," Mrs K corrected her, "this food Kurdish food. We are from Kurdistan."

"Well, whatever it is," Mum smiled, tactfully, "it really is surprisingly good."

There was only one problem: Tulip wouldn't go in the sea. Not properly. I was a good swimmer but

I also loved mucking about and you can't do that on your own. She'd paddle for hours so she wasn't afraid of the water or the cold. It was selfishness, I thought. Dad disagreed: she was sensible! She'd realised how dirty the sea was off Brighton beach. Mum said she probably couldn't swim. When I asked Mrs K, she seemed not to understand. Each evening Tulip promised me that she'd swim tomorrow, and when tomorrow came, she hung her head and wouldn't change out of her clothes.

Halfway through the last week I ducked her. It wasn't deep or dangerous and she was already soaking wet. She screamed when I touched her and people looked up. It couldn't have hurt. I'd only grabbed her shoulders as a joke.

Silently, we climbed back up the beach. I stretched out on the warm pebbles and pretended to fall asleep. Below us the waves shifted the shingle like long, wet hands in a sieve. I wriggled deeper in. I felt shivery despite the high, hot sun. When I woke, I was burning up. I couldn't tell how long I'd been asleep. Tulip was hunched in front of me. I watched her through barely closed lashes. It's a trick I had: people didn't realise I was awake. She was pulling down the neck of her T-shirt, feeling underneath. Below the circle of sunburn I saw the yellowing edge of a huge, purple bruise on her white skin. She glanced back, to check that I was still asleep. Then she lifted another edge. There were more. One, on her shoulder was like a flower. Or teeth on skin. Most had healed but that one had lost its scab. Fresh blood still shone. That was where I'd grabbed her, not knowing what was underneath.

I felt dreadfully sick. Dad was right. Disgusting things were floating in the water. Had I swallowed something as I swam? I rushed to a rubbish bin and threw up. People stared. I threw up again. I was desperate to rest my head. But couldn't, could I? Not on the edge of a bin!

"Down here on your own, are you?" An old woman handed me a tissue. I shook my aching head. "That's good. Because you shouldn't be on your own. Not at your age. Not yet."

I threw up all night and thought my head had split. In the morning the doctor sat on the end of my bed and laughed. She suspected Brighton's busy little friend: salmonella. Had I been eating burgers? Had I been using the loos without washing my hands? I must stay in isolation until she knew the results of her tests. Dad groaned. When Mum said that we should have gone to Turkey, the doctor laughed again.

Later the spike in my brain withdrew. It wasn't salmonella, thank goodness, but I still felt I needed to stay in bed. At first Tulip had hovered. She offered to bring up some games. I shook my head. When she kept on offering I asked her about her back.

"It is nothing," she said.

"How did you do it?" My heart swung in my chest.

"I fall down. I fall with bike on the rocks."

Our eyes met. She was staring at me with her mouth slightly open. I gazed at her perfect teeth. She waited for me to remind her that she hadn't got a bike. But I didn't. I shut my eyes and listened to her going back down the attic steps.

Mum drove me home. Dad drove Tulip and Mrs K. When he'd dropped them off at the hostel, he came up to my room.

"You know she really is a lovely girl," he said.

"She isn't!" I snapped. 'She's as thick as a plank and as dumb as lead!"

◇◇◇

That autumn Mum heard about Polish au pairs. She found Eva, a secondary school teacher, who would do fun stuff with me as well as clean up. Mrs K was told not to come back. In the beginning, Eva and I saw Tulip occasionally in the distance, but I never told Eva who she was. After all, what could I have said? I'd never known anything about her, or why they'd left Turkey, or was it Kurdistan? Jamie had once said that the Karahasans had been driven from their land by the government who was building a dam there, but I've never been interested in things like that.

Then, after my GCSEs, Eva and I went down to Brighton for a week on our own. One afternoon a bunch of crusties and drop-outs scrambled over the breakwater and settled down on the beach. I wanted to move but Eva said that we had a right to be there, so we stayed. They had a young dog on a string and they were teasing him by throwing stones just out of his reach. After an hour or so, one of them got up and dusted the sand from his filthy jeans. He went over to a woman sitting by herself and asked her for money to buy food for his dog. I heard him clearly. The breeze had carried his voice. She'd given him something, then got up and left. He'd approached someone else. Eva was outraged: in her country someone would say something to that lowlife, she said. I prayed that he didn't come to us. And he didn't. A girl came instead.

"No!" Eva shouted. "Go away, you filthy witch! You cannot have my money. You are no better than a thief."

It was Tulip. I'd recognised her as soon as she came close: her lovely leaf green eyes, her perfect, pearly teeth, her chestnut hair, still halfway down her back. But so changed: so thin, so sick. Her hands were encrusted with dirt, her nails bitten further than the quick.

I should have called her back. I should have run

across, emptied my purse, bought her tea, bought her whatever I could, told Eva to shut up, gone for help, called the police. Screamed. I should have done something. Anything. But I didn't. And now it is too late.

I rubbed Eva's cream over my shoulders, then turned on to my stomach and let the sun warm my back.

When I woke Tulip had gone.

Next time, I shall say something. I know I've made a dreadful mistake but I've promised myself that I'll never make this mistake again.

Little Fish
by Kim Kitson

In the 20 years after the Vietnam War ended in 1975, more than one million Vietnamese, mostly Chinese, took to the sea in overcrowded, makeshift boats to escape the new communist government. This reunification of North and South Vietnam began what some historians have called the largest mass exodus of asylum-seekers by sea in modern times. As many as half of these refugees, who came to be known as "the Boat People", drowned, died of illness, dehydration and starvation or were murdered by pirates, police and soldiers. Some children were sent alone: desperate actions for families whose belief in their homeland and ancestors was paramount. Lai Van Huy is a fictional character, but his story is for all those children who made it safely to another life – as well as those who didn't.

Sydney, Australia, 14th February, 1978

It all started with the dark and the running and the boats. The boy lay on the grass beside the river and nudged his paper boat into the current. Now that he lived so far away, he knew the truth about the Vietnam War and the Communists and how, sometimes, you had to run for your life.

Lately, the escape from Vietnam on a fishing boat crammed with strangers had begun to seem like a dream. Huy sighed. But it returned: always on the edge of sleep. He closed his eyes, remembering his old safe game, the one that kept his knees from buckling.

If I count to 50, I am home in the village with Mum and Dad and Grandmother and Grandfather and little Linh and all those noisy cousins. But, now, I am two people forever. He rolled the words across his tongue, "A Vietnamese-Australian."

My-loi, South Vietnam, 20th May, 1977

It hadn't been Huy's idea to go to the pond after lunch. Linh had begged him to float the paper boats. Huy didn't much like water, even though his grandfather always said there was more salt than blood running in his veins what with all the fishermen in the family.

Huy knew First Auntie would put him in charge of all those arguing, hair-pulling cousins. He thought of telling her it hadn't been safe since the soldiers from the north had come to the village. Huy didn't know much about the men in the badly-fitting uniforms. Some of them looked young and hungry, and Huy wondered if that's why they were bad-tempered. He thought if he gave them rice from the shop, they might be happier, but his father had spoken sharply.

"They have their own food, Huy. They are busy checking things, so they don't want to be bothered by 10-year-old boys. Do you understand? They don't like it if you talk to them."

Huy was puzzled, but he nodded. Some grown-ups had seemed pleased about the soldiers. Huy had heard their neighbour say the communists might not be so bad.

"At least they are Vietnamese," he had said.

Huy's father hadn't said anything like that. He hadn't said anything at all. In fact, he had been quiet since his camping trip. His father had left one night without saying goodbye, and he had stayed away for ages. Huy had been used to his father's absences when he worked in the South Vietnamese Army, so he didn't miss him at first. But, later, when he asked his grandmother about it, she had shouted at him and said something about camping and told him to help his mum and his aunties in the shop. Huy sulked for a while, but no one noticed.

Now his father was back, Huy didn't have to work as much, but he wasn't getting as much to eat, either. Dad had always had a big appetite. He used to call his rounded middle his 'prosperous' belly. Though his father was thinner after the camping, Huy was surprised his father wanted to eat so much of his mother's cooking. Her meals had really gone downhill. Yesterday, she had pretended weeds were a type of Chinese cabbage. Huy wondered if the grown-ups had bowls of steaming rice and pork with ginger after the children were put to bed.

It seemed as if most of the village had turned up with their paper boats. Everyone was giddy and mad and loud, and they all staggered about, shouting, trying to sink the other boats.

That night, Huy, with the heat of the day still in him, laughed as his father gathered him out of bed and ran with him through the coconut palms and rubber trees. *A strange midnight game.*

"Why, Daddy?"

His father held a finger to his lips. There was just this running, the tapping and pinching of the rain, and the scuffing of his father's slippers on the ground, and his breath like bellows. Huy closed his eyes against the dark and the slapping wind. He sniffed the air and felt the chill off the river.

Finally, his father slowed. He gestured to Huy to lie flat among the reeds. When he spoke, his voice was torn to pieces on the wind. Then his father's hands were heavy on his shoulders.

"You must be brave, Huy. This is an adventure. The Big Fish will take you to a new life. You will become an Australian. We are all with you."

He traced a finger across the boy's cheek, then whispered, "There is gold hidden in the lining of this shirt." He pressed a gold ring into Huy's palm. "Your mother's."

Huy's father pushed him away, gave him to a stranger, as the wind shrieked above their heads. Huy struggled, scanning the night for his father, but the riverbank was empty. The stranger shoved Huy into the bottom of the boat, into Little Fish, where he lay under a tarpaulin, suffocating with the reek of fish and tangled in legs and bundles.

In the darkness, Huy slipped his jade horse pendant around his neck. He felt calmer with it against his skin, but when he glanced at the other boys, crouched in the circle of their fathers' arms, his stomach burned.

The kids, the shop, the village: that's real.

Before first light, out of the delta, Huy was pressed on to a larger fishing boat. His limbs, cramped into his sides and chest, began to ache and the scratches from the reeds and river grass stung and wept.

On the second night, fights broke out and someone stole the rice cakes his father had tied around his neck. Huy prayed he wouldn't sleep and grunted when his ration of water was handed out for the day.

After four days at sea, no one spoke, though, at night, Huy could hear the murmur of the mothers below deck as they rocked the babies and small children. He felt luckier up on deck. If the boat capsized, he would jump off and swim. Maybe he'd rescue someone; maybe a kid who looked like Linh.

His tears surprised him.

Five babies, a grandmother, a boy and an old man with a cough died that night, their bodies thrown into the sea. Given to the water spirits.

On the fifth day, before sunrise, another boat appeared out of the gloom. People called out between the vessels, hope beating in faces thin with sickness and grief. They shouted the names of their villages and the countries they dreamed about.

The boats limped on together, bracing themselves against the storm. Huy rubbed his eyes, weeping from the sun and the salt. There had been no land for two days and, at times, the boy wasn't sure where the sky was separated from the sea.

When the waves began to suck across the deck, Huy dropped into the press of bodies below the railing. He began to count: his safe game, thinking of everyone in turn, completing the circle of his family.

The fishing boat shook and slammed into the heart of the storm. A boy clutched at Huy's arm, raking the skin and tearing his shirt from his back. Huy reached for him, but the boy slid out of his grasp, tumbling across brothers and sons and fathers and uncles and grandfathers, careering right to the railing, which surrendered to the wind and the water, the boy's mouth a question mark as the sea reached up to swallow him. Huy covered his eyes, held his breath. The day cracked open.

The mast of the other boat snapped like a matchstick, and the waves shook the people from the deck. The water churned with bodies and the people's screams carried on the wind. Then, nothing.

Huy's boat rocked slightly. From below deck, the women's chanting seeped into the dawn, weeping through the souls huddled together on the empty ocean.

Huy sat shirtless. He threaded his pendant and the gold ring through the cord of his shorts. Everything else was lost to the sea.

The grandfather next to Huy nudged him, passed him a sticky sweet. "It's lemon and ginseng, keep the water flowing in your mouth."

The boy offered up his palms in a steeple of thanks. The old man grunted. "Where is your family?"

"My father ran through the forest to the river."

The old man nodded. Huy thought of his own grandfather.

"My family are still at home," and Huy shook his head, bewildered. One day playing, one day running for his life. He wondered when he would go home.

"You must be brave," the old man said. "You will be the first seed in the ground. You will become a strong tree."

Hours later, as Huy pushed the tip of his tongue

at the sliver of sweet, someone stood, shouting and pointing at the horizon: a floating island, as grey as the sky. Huy's boat trailed in the navy ship's wake until darkness fell. The boy was certain they were lost, a speck on the eye of the world.

Hope crept up on the boat people. They awoke to see the giant of the day before looming over them. Men in uniforms called down to them in English, Chinese, French and Vietnamese. The frigate escorted Huy's boat into the bay of what looked like an island, though Huy couldn't be sure. When he heard the men talking about Malaysia, Huy was astonished. He felt sure they must be close to Australia.

"It's a camp," someone explained.

Huy nodded. Not knowing, thinking of his father. Perhaps he came here. Maybe that's why he was gone so long. Huy jiggled into a standing position.

A long wharf, like a needle, stretched over the beach. At the end, a sign proclaimed PULAU BIDONG and, past that, a tide of people flowed back and forth, kicking up a pall of dust, which cloaked the buildings and hung in the trees.

The processing office was small, stinking. Huy squeezed his arms tight against his sides and licked his lips. The ceiling fan wasn't working, though he could hear the generator choking behind the cabin. The men opposite him were flushed, the white man's voice damp and tired.

Huy tapped his foot. The translator frowned and Huy dropped his eyes. No one was surprised about him being on his own. They had plucked lone 10-year-olds off boats before, but the translator told Huy it was better to say he was 12 or 13. It would be easier to be granted asylum. Huy breathed in, hoping no one could hear the hammering in his chest. He was shaking, his knee tapping again.

A loudspeaker crackled in the central courtyard, and Huy joined the throng. There, in the squeeze of families, for once Huy's stomach didn't ache. He sat down and half closed his eyes. A hand shook his arm.

"Hey! Ugly! Where are you from?"

Huy jumped, felt the jade horse slap against his heart. A scrawny girl about his age, toddler on her hip, was glaring at him.

"I said..." she stared at his pendant, " ...where are you from, horse boy? Saigon?"

Huy shook his head. The girl's little sister struggled down and crouched in front of him, reaching for his pendant. Startled by her likeness to Linh, Huy smiled.

"What's your sister's name?" he asked.

"Binh. I'm Ha. Where are your parents?"

Huy hacked at the dirt in front of him, spraying the fine dust into his eyes. When he had rubbed the muck clear, the girls had gone. He shrugged: *back to their family*. Huy found a spot under a tree and waited for the call to lunch.

Again, the shake on his arm. "You've come on your own, haven't you?" Ha dragged him to his feet. "Where are you going?"

Huy stared at her, amazed. *Stupid Girl.*

"Australia, of course."

"What do you mean, 'of course'?"

"My father said."

"Okay." The girl's eyes slid over his too-large charity shirt, his tattered shorts and bare feet. "You know you're a refugee, don't you?"

"A what? No. I'm from South Vietnam, from My-loi. I've been sent ahead on an adventure. My father probably didn't know the boat trip would be so crowded, or there would be storms. He paid a lot of money. My father told me I wouldn't ever really be alone, but I have been and I lost all the treasure except for my mother's heirloom."

Huy paused. Someone was crying.

"When my parents get to Australia, we can go camping. My father sometimes goes by himself and in Australia we'll see snow and kangaroos like in the books. Then we'll go home."

He held his hands in front of his wet face.

The bossy girl coughed a couple of times.

"Look horse boy, this isn't a holiday camp. I'll look after you. Everyone's a little fish here."

Someone had dubbed the camp 'mini-Saigon', and with Ha and her shadow, baby Binh, whom he sometimes called Linh, Huy soon knew every corner of it. The girls' parents seemed to accept him easily enough. Huy slept at the end of their bunk, next to Ha's snorting father.

Sometimes, when he and Ha were supposed to be in school learning English and Binh was asleep with her mother, Huy would slip away to the temple to make offerings and burn incense for his family. Once, he hunkered down in a doorway and pretended he could hear his mother calling him in for lunch. But, as the weeks passed, Huy found it increasingly difficult to keep his parents' faces in his head.

At night, he haunted the shops. People slipped him pieces of fish and vegetable scraps. He shared these with Ha's family, but he kept the sweet treats for Binh. Every day, he searched for the old man from the boat. After a week, the boy wondered if he had imagined him.

Sometimes, Huy was startled out of sleep by dreams filled with screams, thudding flesh and running feet. On these nights, he lay in the smothering dark, his heart slamming, his mouth dry. Once, he saw Ha staring at the roof, her fingers in her ears. When Binh woke, he would sing the soft songs of his childhood. When she cried, he gave her his jade horse to chew on.

◇◇◇

"Lai Van Huy!"

His name was called in his third month in the camp. The loudspeaker had been droning into the morning and each time a name was called out, the groups shifted and shuffled in the dust. Ha dug him in the ribs.

"It's you, idiot. You're free to go. You can be an Australian now."

Huy felt rather stern. "I'd rather go home."

"OK, OK. I know." She flicked her fingers at him. "Maybe I'll take your place."

The girl dashed to a spot under a tree.

Huy chased her. "What's up?"

"You're going, and Binh's sick. No country will take a family with a sick person. We have to wait."

Huy would miss Ha, but his own family was relying on him. He tutted.

"My little sister Linh was always getting sick, too, and she's fine now. Well, she doesn't speak." He blinked.

Ha shook her head at her friend. "Huy. I've been thinking about all those people whose names will never be called."

When Huy woke the next morning, Ha's family had already gone to breakfast. He stretched out, relishing the space, and let the morning seep into his bones. *No more lining up for food, no more rotten vegetables and fish*. Huy felt anything was possible.

He looked around. The bedding was strewn across the bunks.

Ha's mother is strict about tidying up.

Sweat prickled over the boy's body. He sat bolt upright. Huy didn't like things out of place. He tried to do the same things in the same way every day.

They must have slept in, too. Probably rushing.

He knew it wasn't true.

The family wasn't in the kitchen. Huy checked the shops, the courtyard, the school. *Where else? There's nowhere.*

Huy squinted into the sun, which was still low in the sky. He tried to think. His mouth dry, his head full of heat.

I didn't oversleep. I just slept well. There was no snoring. There wasn't anything.

Huy sprinted to the temple. His feet clattered at the door, the echo swinging through the stillness.

"Because of the heat, bodies are to be buried immediately. No observances. THANK YOU." Yesterday's order had hung in the air.

Huy knew. He knew in the squeeze of his heart. He ran through the undergrowth and into the forest beyond the camp, pain knifing into his gut. At the clearing, he vomited, wiped his mouth with the back of his hand, staring at the disturbed earth.

Huy found Binh at the edge of the forest: a tiny

footprint in the wilderness, far from her ancestors. He straightened the splintery marker, read the simple inscription, shook as he knelt.

I forgot my safe game.

Huy cried as he counted. He counted and counted and counted, even though he knew it didn't always keep everyone safe.

The long boat that would take Huy away from the camp was already ferrying refugees across the water for the bus to Kuala Lumpur. Huy found Ha sitting on the beach with her back to the camp, watching the newest arrivals stumble out of the water. He reached out and pressed his mother's gold ring into her palm.

He wanted to say something about the circle of life, but he hadn't been praying much and he couldn't remember if it was Buddha or his father or his grandfather or the old man on the boat or what his grandmother said the ancestors in the jars had said. Anyway, he just couldn't and it didn't sound right in his head and he didn't want to cry again or make Ha angry with him and he knew the ring was treasure and might be enough for a new life.

"Good luck, bossy girl," he managed.

At the wharf, Huy looked back and raised a hand in farewell. He started. Behind Ha, in the shade of a tree, was the old man from the boat. He had been here all the time.

Sydney, Australia, 25th February, 1978

Huy sat up and brushed the dirt from his school shirt. Huy craved this solitude, tired as he was by the dragging vowels, the nicknames, the strangeness of the food, the city and its inhabitants. Actually, he didn't mind the nicknames. In Vietnam, his grandmother called him much worse names to keep away the bad spirits, to keep him safe.

He took the letter from his top pocket. It had arrived yesterday, and when he read it out to Jack's mother, her face had creased with tears. Huy knew it by heart. His family was on their way. They had sold everything they owned, piece by piece until they had enough gold hidden to build their own boat with three other families. After four days, the engine blew up but Huy's father somehow fixed it and they trudged on to Malaysia. In the camp, Grandfather had fallen sick, and Huy's mother said they couldn't apply to Australia until he was better.

Huy shivered. He watched his paper boat ride the sudden ripple. He began to count: his safe game. The little boat's sail dipped. Through the hedge, he could hear kids shouting. His foster brother Jack would be there with his new football. Huy strode to the gate, paused, looked back over his shoulder.

Still afloat.

He could see Jack on the other side. He thought of the village and his family in the camp. He thought of Ha and Binh. He pushed his way through the hedge and out into the school field.

Jack waved. "Huy. We need you."

The boy hesitated. The letter crackled in his top pocket. Huy ran. Under the cloudless Australian sky, Huy ran and ran and ran. He kicked and passed. His shadow was long in the afternoon and his jade horse, dark green and strong, twisted and slammed against his heart.

Give Me Shelter
by Solomon Gebremedhin

This story is based on what so many young people had to go through when a dictator government in Ethiopia known as Derg was in power. Children were kidnapped from streets and forced to be soldiers. A huge number of these children had no choice but to run away to neighbouring countries such as Sudan where they claimed asylum.

I remember the last night I spent with my mother. I was hiding under her bed, praying that the police wouldn't find me. Outside the house I heard voices, quiet and hushed, and then loud and angry. They were searching for Ethiopian boys. They wanted to force us to be soldiers but I didn't want to fight for this horrible regime. I was just 12 years old and I wanted to stay with Mum. I lay shaking and shivering with fear, wishing that I could magically disappear to a place where no one could find me.

When the police had gone, my mother came into the room. I crept out from under the bed. Her eyes were red and puffy. I saw the sadness in her face.

"Danny, you must go to the secret place. You know the one I mean," she whispered. "It is not safe for you here. Hide there until tomorrow morning, and I will bring you something to eat."

103

I pulled on my trainers, said goodbye to my mother and crept out of the front door into the night. You were forbidden to be outside after 8pm unless you had a very good reason. It was 11pm and I knew that if the police or soldiers found me, I would be in big trouble. I knew that I couldn't hide for ever from the government. One day soon they would find me and I would be forced to kill for them – to become one of the people I feared the most.

I followed the path to the mountains. I had walked that way so many times. I used to fetch water from the streams that ran down the mountainsides – but that was before my father was taken.

Dad was a teacher in the local secondary school. He taught economics and politics. He belonged to a party which strongly opposed the terrible Derg Regime. One day, when my father was teaching, the police came to the school and took him. We never saw or heard from him again. Mum and I knew that he must be dead but we always hoped he might come back to us one day.

I had been walking for about fifteen minutes when I spotted a light coming towards me. I couldn't see who it was but I knew that it must be soldiers. I felt a horrible feeling of panic rising from my belly into my throat. My head felt hot. I tried to calm down and think what to do. All around me, the land was littered with rubbish. I crept over to one of the piles and lay down next to it, pressing my body as close to the earth as I could. I hoped that the soldiers wouldn't notice me lying there. I could feel the blood racing through my body and my heart seemed to beat so loudly, I was sure the men would hear it. They didn't. They walked right past me, talking loudly and laughing. I waited for a few minutes until I couldn't see or hear them, then brushed myself off and carried on walking.

There was a little cave hidden in the side of one of the mountains. It was my secret place. My friends and I had played there many times. As I drew close I heard voices. Sami and Babi were hiding there too! None of us wanted to be soldiers. We all wanted the freedom to be who we wanted to be, not to end up in a nameless grave.

Sami was one of my best friends. He was 13. A year earlier the police had killed his two big brothers. They were in a protest march against the government and the police opened fire on the crowd. Hardly anyone survived. My other friend, Babi, was also 13. He knew a lot about politics and he wanted to live in the United States of America.

I was so pleased to see them. I slumped down on a rock and started to cry.

"What's wrong, Danny?" asked Babi. I told him all about the police coming to our house, the soldiers and the dark, scary walk to the cave.

Mum arrived very early the next morning with a big water bucket. Hidden inside was some fresh bread and a delicious chicken sauce. Sami, Babi and I sat down to eat. My stomach was turning over and over with hunger.

"Oh, boys. I wish you were all little girls," Mum sighed.

"Why?" we asked.

"It's not safe for young boys like you in Ethiopia any more," she said. "One day soon, the police will find you and take you away."

For a while Mum was silent. She looked at each of us as we ate. Then she said, "I have a very important thing to discuss with you. I have spoken to Sami and Babi's mothers and they agree that you boys cannot stay in Ethiopia. You must escape across the border to Sudan. We will give you some money."

I felt my heart stop.

"Be ready to leave at 8pm tonight," Mum said. "We will come to say goodbye. Stay hidden in this cave until we arrive. I will cough twice, so you know it is us."

After Mum had left, we sat huddled together. We were too shocked and scared to talk about what might happen to us. We just sat in silence, as the heat of the day turned into dusk, and then darkness.

At 8pm we heard two little coughs, and three sad-looking figures drew closer to the cave entrance. One of them was my mother.

"It's time to leave," sobbed Sami's mother. She handed us a plastic bag. "This food should last for a few days."

We all nodded our heads. We didn't say anything. All we felt was a deep sadness settle in our hearts that would stay with us for ever.

I had never been away from my family, except for once when I was six years old. Mum sent me to stay with Dad's family for a few days. I cried every day and wouldn't eat or play. When Mum came to fetch me, I was overjoyed to see her. But this time there would be no going home for me.

"What will happen to us?" I asked.

"You must be brave," said Mum. "You must get across the border. That is the most important thing."

I felt Mum's arms around me but I couldn't hear what she was saying. It all seemed so unreal, like a terrible dream.

So Sami, Babi and I left our childhood home behind us and walked towards the border of Sudan. None of us spoke. Our hearts were torn in two. This dangerous place we were leaving behind was our home, our beautiful country.

For days we walked through the bush. We were tired, hungry and thirsty and our food supply was low. Then one day, we came across a lorry driver on the side of the road. His little cab pulled four containers behind it. It was hot and the engine needed water to keep cool. We helped him to find a stream, hoping he might help us cross the border.

The driver tried to give us money.

"No thank you, sir," said Babi. "We don't want money. Please will you help us to cross the border into Sudan?"

"I'm sorry," said the driver. "Do you know what will happen to me if you are discovered? I cannot take that risk."

I was filled with dread. Perhaps we would never get across the border! We begged the driver to reconsider but he refused and drove off.

Miserably, we carried on walking along the road towards Sudan. But then we heard the sound of the tanker's engines once more. The driver had turned round!

He leaned out of the cab.

"I've changed my mind, boys. I want to help you," he said.

"Thank you so much," we stammered.

The driver gave us water and hid us in one of the lorry's containers. It was so cramped, we could hardly move. It was hard to breathe and we were still several hours' drive from the Sudanese border. My back and bottom ached and my legs were cramped. The road was rough and full of holes. Each time one of the tanker's wheels hit a hole, we were thrown into the air for a moment before bouncing back again. The driver drove very quickly and we were hot and very uncomfortable.

Then the lorry stopped. Sami, Babi and I looked at each other in fear. We knew so many people didn't make it to Sudan because there was something wrong with their legal documents – and we didn't even have any! But I calmed myself by remembering how brave we were leaving our home and families to escape a terrible future. Time passed slowly – 5 minutes, 10 minutes, 20 minutes – and still the lorry didn't move. I could hear voices approaching the lorry, footsteps coming towards our container... and then the lorry started moving!

"Thank God," said Sami, shakily.

I couldn't say a word. My heart was pounding and my body was shivering with relief. I felt as though I was suddenly alone in a big, empty ocean.

When the lorry stopped again, the driver opened the container and we tumbled out, stretching our stiff arms and legs. We were in Sudan and behind us lay beautiful, troubled Ethiopia. I looked back toward my homeland and felt sad but then I felt the strong spirit of my mother pushing me on, giving me hope.

"I am going to Khartoum," the driver said. We knew that was the capital city of Sudan. "You boys can travel with me if you like."

We all nodded gratefully and climbed up into the driver's cab.

"Right, let's get going, boys," said the driver, and we set off towards our new life.

◇ ◇ ◇

Three months later, Sami, Babi and I were living in Khartoum. We all had jobs but the pay was very low because we were illegal immigrants. I wanted to send some of my wages home to Mum but I couldn't. I didn't have any ID so I couldn't open a bank account. I worked in a shop for a wonderful and kind man called Mustafa. He came from Saudi Arabia. Every day when I woke, I thanked God for making me so lucky.

One morning I woke up dazed and confused. A woman with a baby was sitting next to me. I wondered if I was having a nightmare.

"Are you all right?" the woman asked me.

I nodded and looked around. I was in a small boat in the open sea. I couldn't remember how I got there. Was I dreaming? The deck was packed with people all squashed together. There was no room to move. Nearby was a woman wearing a headscarf and a long black dress that covered her whole body. I could only see her eyes watching me.

"Excuse me," I said to her, "where is the toilet?"

She pointed to the only toilet on the ship. It was filthy. I moved towards it. What had happened? Where was I? Why was I covered in bruises? I knew

I had to try and remember.

As I sat on the toilet, my head began to clear.

◇ ◇ ◇

At first, my life in Sudan was happy, except for missing my mother. Mustafa was a kind man and I liked his wife, Amina.

When we first met, Amina was nice to me but as time wore on she began to look at me suspiciously. She watched everything I did in the shop. I didn't say anything. I wanted her to see that I wouldn't steal from them. I just wanted to work and be useful. I told Babi about Amina but he told me not to worry.

When I got back to my room at night I would stitch my money into the sole of my trainers. I had no bank account, so I needed to carry my money with me at all times. One night I came back from work so tired that I lay down on my bed. I couldn't even be bothered to take off my shoes.

Suddenly there was a bang at door, like someone trying to smash the wood to pieces. The door burst open and someone came in. He struck me on the face. The world began to grow dim. The pain was too much for my head. I collapsed in a faint.

When I woke up, I was in prison. My whole body was hurting and I was covered in cuts and bruises.

"Why I am being held here?" I asked the guard.

"For stealing money from your employer," he answered.

Who would accuse me of such a terrible thing? Not Mustafa. He trusted me and I would never have stolen from him. It must have been Amina!

"God knows the truth," I said to the guard.

I had no solicitor and I was an illegal immigrant. If Amina convinced the judge that I had stolen money from them, I would have my hand chopped off. I would also be sentenced to life in prison or get the death penalty. I was innocent! But who would believe an illegal immigrant against the word of a respected citizen? I would have to escape. I had to get to Europe or America – but how? I didn't even have a piece of paper to say who was!

Escaping from prison was easier than I thought. It was too hot to keep the prisoners indoors so we slept outside. The guards carried swords and they drugged our food and water. I couldn't have escaped without Sami and Babi's help. I waited until the guards were busy with another prisoner and then I ran away. Sami and Babi, my true brothers, gave me some money and lent me a camel.

I rode to the port. I was very sad to leave my two friends, but I had no choice.

◇ ◇ ◇

So there I was, inside a stinking toilet on a boat to France. I walked back to where I had been sleeping. I didn't smile or look at anyone. There was very little to eat and the children were crying. I ate a few dates and some stale bread. The drinking water tasted salty. After many days we arrived in France, sick, hungry and tired.

I was told that I should head for Britain. There were many people from Ethiopia there and I might get help from them. Eventually I was given a ticket on a boat leaving for the port of Dover. I was so happy to see England! I saw a notice in my language advising me to claim asylum as soon as possible. As I waited for the immigration people to see me, I wondered if this new country would be safe. Here I was with no friends or family. I couldn't speak the language. I hoped that God would not abandon me now.

A nice lady led me into a room and several people interviewed me for hours. They asked a lot of difficult questions and I was very miserable. All I wanted was something to eat and a bed to sleep in.

I was taken to a children's home in Kent. It was a home for British children and many of them had also had a hard time. Some of the children picked on me because of my black skin.

"Go back to Africa. You don't belong here," said one girl. This made me very sad.

◇ ◇ ◇

Then I was sent to a foster home and I started to go to school. Slowly I began to make new friends.

So here I am. I am still waiting to hear if the Home Office will allow me to stay. I don't know how long this journey will last. I only hope that one day I will be able to see my mother again and visit the land where I was born.

Cherry Strudel
by Leslie Wilson

During the 1990s Yugoslavia fell apart as a country, and there were terrible wars between its various regions and peoples, particularly in Croatia and Bosnia. In the late 1990s there was more fighting in Kosovo, a place where most of the people were Albanian. Many were killed, and like Jusuf, even more fled the country, seeking refuge elsewhere...

He was running up to the goal, and the other players were trying to get the ball off him. But his footwork was way too good for them and he sent the ball soaring towards the goal posts that he'd chalked on the wall at the end of the garden.

The crowd's roar was ringing in his ears. "Asllani! Asllani!" Then the ball hit the corner of the wall, bounced off at an angle, flew into the garden next door and...

Smash! Oh no! It had hit the greenhouse.

"Jusuf! Jusuf Asllani!"

It wasn't a lot of people shouting his name now. It was just Mrs Macdonald. Old Her Next Door.

He had to get away. Out through the garden gate into the back lane. As he ran he shoved his earpieces in and put his music on. Loud.

He couldn't hear her now. He pushed out of the

back gate into the lane and pulled his hood up, right over his face. That felt safer. He was running really fast, feeling his legs pumping him along to the beat of the music. He was an athlete at the Olympics. That was cool.

He was almost at the end of the lane when he heard the shots. Three of them, one after another. He dropped like a stone and lay still, his heart thumping.

"Get up, boy! What's wrong with you?"

Old Her Next Door's voice. He felt sick. It had happened again. And it had only been a car backfiring. Why had he thought it was guns?

His music had stopped. Maybe he'd broken his personal stereo when he went down.

He stood up, pulling his hood round his face. His knees were hurting.

"Are you all right, Jusuf?" Old Her Next Door sounded worried now. Why? She should be angry with him for smashing a hole in her greenhouse. There was a battery lying among the broken black tarmac chunks of the lane. His battery, out of his personal stereo.

That was why it wasn't working.

She frowned. "Listen to me, Jusuf. You've broken my greenhouse roof. I can't ask your aunt to pay for the repairs, she has troubles enough."

"Leave me alone," he muttered.

She said, "Why do you have to make things

worse for her?"

She had an accent when she spoke English. That was because she was German, even though she had a Scottish name from her husband. He was dead now. Probably living with her had killed him.

He put the battery in his pocket and ran off.

◇ ◇ ◇

Running was all right, you kept leaving everything behind you. At school, running was the only thing he was good at. Not football. He only liked playing football on his own.

In painting lessons, though, things sometimes got all loud inside him, like music. Then he'd grab the brush and paint something huge and bright and splashy. But the colours went dull when the paint dried. It wasn't the same then. Mr Stanley put it up on the wall and said it was 'powerful'. He was stupid. He couldn't see how useless the dead dry paint was.

His group tutor, Miss Knox, had tried to get him to talk to the class about his 'homeland'. He'd said no. "But Jusuf," she'd said, "people want to understand. And we all know about the war, and how the Serbs attacked your people. We'd like to hear how you feel."

"No," he'd said.

She said, "Aren't you lonely, Jusuf?"

He started jigging up and down on his feet, looking anywhere but at her, and then he knocked a book off her desk and she got angry and gave up on him.

He didn't want anyone – not anyone – asking him questions. That was one reason he didn't hang out with the other kids.

Tom Harrison was all right. Tom didn't take any notice of him most of the time, but sometimes he'd come up at home-time and then they'd go to each other's houses and play computer games. Car-racing games. He couldn't stand the ones where people got shot.

Tom never asked questions. They just got on with playing the games.

◇ ◇ ◇

He came in through the garden gate and skulked up to the kitchen door so Old Her Next Door wouldn't see him. Aunty Julja was home from work. He could see her through the glass panels in the kitchen door. She was taking boxes out of a plastic Lidl bag. He hoped it was pizza. And Vjoleta was there and she was going on about him. As usual.

"It must have been Jusuf, he's always kicking his ball into her garden. There's a great big hole in one of the panes. Mum, he's awful. You're too soft on him, because of what happened, but – look, it was horrible for us, too –"

"Don't," Aunty Julja said in an odd voice. "You know I can't bear it."

Jusuf wanted to run, but he banged his elbow into the door as he was turning round. Aunty Julja turned round and saw him.

"Jusuf!" she said, as if she was glad to have him to be angry with. "Come in! Right now!"

The kitchen was really narrow, it was a squeeze for the three of them. He said, "Wow! Pizza!"

"Jusuf," Aunty Julja said, "did you break the glass in Mrs Macdonald's greenhouse?"

"Did she say I did?"

"Jusuf, I haven't got time to play around. I've got to go out again after dinner, there's a meeting."

She was always working. She was supposed to be part-time at the Refugee Support Group, but there were meetings in the evenings and people rang her up at home all the time.

He dodged round her, trying to see what flavour pizzas she'd brought.

"Jusuf," she said, trying to take hold of him and keep him still.

"It was an accident," he muttered, twisting away from her. "It's all right, she won't ask you to pay for it. Oh, cool! Ham and pineapple!"

Vjoleta said, "Don't you understand anything? We'll have to pay for it."

He said, "She doesn't want you to."

"Yes," Aunty Julja said. "She said that because she's a good woman. Look at how she helped us learn English when we came here, have you forgotten that?"

"Yes," he said. "She bossed us all about."

Mrs Macdonald had white cards in a plastic bag and a roll of Sellotape and she'd gone round the house as if she owned it, writing on the cards with a thick black marker pen – TELEVISION, COOKER, FRIDGE, BATH, BED, CUPBOARD – and sticking the cards on the furniture. She said each word out loud and they'd had to repeat it. He'd messed around and said the words wrong on purpose. She'd looked disapprovingly at him over the tops of her half-glasses.

Aunty Julja frowned at him. "It would be wrong of me not to pay for the damage."

He said, "The cards kept falling off on to the floor and we put them back on the wrong things."

"You did," said Vjoleta, giving him a bad look.

He said, "The one on the cooker caught on fire." Then he ran upstairs to his Playstation.

That night he had the dream again.

◇ ◇ ◇

There was somebody pounding on the house door. He was in Kosovo. Nobody went to open the door because they knew who it was. Jusuf's heart was hammering with fright and his mouth was dry as paper. Mum had her arm round him, holding him tight and the shivers jolted them like a train. The Serbs were smashing the door down.

The Serbs were their neighbours, all men they knew. Mr Nikolic was one of the first to trample over the wrecked door, kicking a bit of wood away.

Jusuf wanted to shout out, "But Mr Nikolic, we're your friends! You and Dad and Grandad and Uncle Bujar used to sit in the café laughing and joking. Didn't you? And if I came by, you used to say: 'Hello, young man,' and ruffle my hair up."

But when he looked at Mr Nikolic he wondered if he'd only imagined those things, because you could see from Mr Nikolic's face that he hated them all.

All the men and the boys in the village were out on the street and they herded Dad and Jusuf and his big brother Florjan in with them. Uncle Bujar was there, with Vjoleta's brothers, Dren and Ibrahim, and Grandad.

"Put your hands on the backs of your heads," Mr Nikolic shouted. "Move!"

They started to walk awkwardly forward and the guns cracked. Jusuf felt as if something hot had burned his shoulder. All the other men fell down. Jusuf fell down too. He didn't decide to do it. He just went flat. Suddenly he heard Mum screaming.

She was running over to them, shrieking "No! No!" Someone else was running too, but shakily. That was Granny. The guns cracked again and he heard them fall. All the while Jusuf lay so still he thought he must be dead too. He just couldn't move. Then he smelt smoke.

After a while he heard women's voices wailing. His eyes opened in spite of himself. He felt dizzy and his shoulder was hurting. He saw Aunty Julja and Vjoleta and he called out to them. They came running to him and helped him up.

All the rest of the boys and men were dead. Mum and Granny had been shot dead, too. And the street was filling with smoke and they had to get away and leave everyone else behind, or they'd choke.

Now he started to yell and struggle. "I don't want to remember! I don't want to remember!"

He was awake. He was back in England, and it was morning.

He got out of bed and opened up his Playstation. He raced the computer car round and round the track. Nobody could catch him.

◇ ◇ ◇

Jusuf went downstairs and ate a bowl of Coco-Pops. Then he heard voices in the garden. Aunty Julja and Vjoleta were arguing with Old Her Next

Door. He opened the kitchen door so he could listen properly.

It was about the greenhouse. Aunty Julja wanted to pay for the repair.

"It was my nephew who smashed your glass," she said.

Old Her Next Door said, "Mrs Asllani, I should have got the whole greenhouse reglazed years ago. With safety glass."

Vjoleta said, "You're only getting the new glass because of Jusuf."

"That's not true," said Old Her Next Door.

Aunty Julja turned round suddenly, saw Jusuf, and called out, "Do you hear this? Mrs Macdonald thinks I'm so poor I can't afford to pay for one pane of glass. And you just stand there, listening..."

Jusuf was furious all of a sudden. He ran out into the garden and said, "I – I'll make it up to her."

The three of them turned round and stared at him.

"Her?" Aunty Julja said. "Where are your manners?"

"All right," he said. "To Mrs Macdonald."

"What will you do, Jusuf?" Old Her Next Door said.

For a moment his mind was just a blank, then he said the first thing that came into his head.

"I'll help you in your garden."

She stood still and frowned.

Vjoleta butted in. "Mrs Macdonald wouldn't want *you* messing up her garden. You knew that, you said it so you could get out of it."

"I didn't," he said. "I didn't."

Vjoleta shrieked, "You did. You're lazy. All you ever do is play computer games, and look at you now, I bet you haven't washed…"

Jusuf wanted to throw his cereal at her. And he was almost crying. That was horrible.

"Jusuf!" Aunty Julja started saying, but Mrs Macdonald interrupted her.

"Mrs Asllani," she said. "I accept Jusuf's offer."

They all stared at her.

"I have to go shopping," Mrs Macdonald said, "so come round at eleven, Jusuf, and I'll show you what to do."

"You'll be no good," Vjoleta said in her '*I'm better than you*' voice. "If she sets you to weeding, you'll pull up all her flowers."

Aunty Julja frowned. "Mrs Macdonald loves her garden, Jusuf. I hope you don't ruin it for her."

"I won't," he said, and went up to play car-racing.

❖ ❖ ❖

He couldn't believe the next door garden was just the same size as his. It seemed much bigger just because there was so much in it. There was a rose growing over the gate, and a path with green stuff growing between the stones, and clumps of flowers and bushes growing up either side of the path like a forest. One of them had big white flowers that smelt good. He went under an arch with a blue trailing flower growing over it. It was all really nice till he saw the greenhouse with the smashed pane in its roof and Her Next Door standing beside it. Then it felt awful.

"I want you to wash plant pots for me," she said. "Can you bring those up to the house?" She pointed to a stack of plastic pots, all different sizes.

She had paving at the back of the house, and a metal table and chairs so she could sit out and eat. She put washing-up liquid in the bucket, filled it up with water from the outside tap, and handed him an old washing-up brush with a splayed, faded head. He had to use that to wash the pots with the soapy water and then he had to pour the water out on a thing with big silvery leaves like a thistle to kill the black flies that were spoiling it.

That reminded him of something from home, something he didn't want to remember because it hurt. The curve of bubbly water pouring out on to green leaves so that the whole plant was foamy. Dad laughing and saying, "We're shampooing the plants."

No, Jusuf thought. He had the pots to wash, that was what he had to think about. At least she didn't stay there and watch him.

"Come and tell me when you've finished," she said, and went into the kitchen.

There must have been fifty plant pots and the bits of dry earth stuck hard to some of them. It took a long time. When he'd done all the pots he emptied out the water over the silvery plant and went into her house to tell her. She didn't have a little kitchen like there was in their house. There was just one big room downstairs. She was sitting at a round table, cutting black cherries in half and putting them into a bowl.

"Have one," she said.

He ate the cherry and spat the stone into his hand. Then he put it in the plastic container with all the other stones and stalks in it.

Her hands were all black with cherry juice. When he saw them he felt odd and wobbly inside, because of Mum's black hands when she made jam. Mum's cherry jam – *no*, he thought, slamming the memory out of his mind. *No*.

Old Her Next Door went out and inspected the pots. "You've washed these well," she said. She sounded relieved, as if she'd been afraid he'd make a mess of it. Well, he hadn't, had he? Then she filled the bucket up with clear water. Did she think he couldn't turn a tap on without breaking it?

"Now rinse them all out," she said. "If the water gets soapy, get another bucketful. But don't waste the water. Pour it on the hydrangea," she pointed to a bush with flowers that looked like lace. "It likes a lot of water."

So he had to rinse all the soap off the pots. It wasn't as bad as last time, but he didn't want to leave any foam on any of them. The foam looked a bit like the hydrangea flowers.

When he went in again she had a tablecloth on the table and was pulling at a thin sheet of pastry. She was making filo pastry. Aunty Julja made that when she had time, but when she was too busy she bought it from the shop.

"Are you cooking cheese pies?" he asked.

"No," she said. "Cherry strudel. If you work well you can have some when you've finished." She had her hands underneath the sheet of pastry and was tugging it gently outward. Then she clicked her tongue. "I've made a hole. And it's still not thin enough. My mother used to say you ought to be able to read the newspaper through it."

She stopped, brushed melted butter over the pastry, and went outside with him again. This time she told him to move all the plants out of her greenhouse and bring them to the sitting-out place in front of the house.

She had tomatoes and peppers growing in pots. He took the peppers out first, they were small plants, so that was easy. The tomatoes were at the back, and they were up to his waist already.

He worried they might topple over when he carried them. They smelt good! When he smelt that earthy green smell it felt as if there was someone standing beside him, whispering to him, "Do you remember what it was like, eating tomatoes off the plant with them all warm from the sun? Dad's tomatoes weren't hard and cold like the tomatoes here that come out of the fridge, they tasted so good." And he saw the garden at home as if he was there. The big leaves of cucumbers and watermelons and the curved fruit glinting as it lay on the earth. Feathery carrot-tops and square white potato-flowers with little yellow blobs in the middle of them. And roses.

Only then he smelt smoke. Smoke from two years ago in Kosovo. The smoke of his home burning up.

He clenched his whole self together till the bad smell went away a bit. Not altogether. Just a bit. Then he went in to Her Next Door.

"I've taken all the plants out."

There was a lumpy roll of pastry sitting on the tablecloth. The lumps must be the cherries inside the pastry. The kitchen was hot because the oven was on.

She said, "Jusuf. Will you help me with the strudel? I can't get it off the tablecloth on to the baking tray all on my own."

So he held the black baking tray steady and held his breath while she eased the lumpy roll forward off the tablecloth. It was so huge, no wonder it was difficult. Kosovan cheese pies were neat little parcels.

It would fall forward on to the tray any moment. It'd be heavy. She'd be really angry if he let it drop. *Flop*! It was on the tray, lying there like a dead fish.

"Good," she said. "Thank you, Jusuf." She pushed a hand into her wiry white hair and smiled for a moment. It was even a nice smile.

He said, "I've got all the plants out of the greenhouse. What do you want me to do now?"

She put the tray into the oven and then went out into the garden with him. She looked around, as if she didn't know what she could tell him to do.

"I could pull up some weeds for you," he said.

She didn't say anything. Then she said, "Show me which plants you think are weeds."

He saw a weed that climbed up and strangled other plants – he didn't know the English name. It was all round a climbing rose.

"I could get that out," he said.

"The bindweed? All right. But only that. Don't pull anything else up."

"Yes," he muttered.

It was a horrible, scratchy job, pulling it off the rose. And all the time the memories were trying to come back. They were hammering at the door he'd put up against them in his mind. He wanted to run, but he couldn't. He had to stay here and do this job properly. He didn't know why that was so important, but it was.

The old woman was calling him. "Jusuf! Come and have some strudel!"

She'd got a can of coke for him and she'd made coffee for herself. There was a slice of the strudel-thingy on a plate for each of them, with a dollop of cream. It lay there and it looked nice now, with a mixture of cherries and nuts lying inside a thin roll of pastry. There was powdery icing sugar lying on the plate round it. She'd given him a fork to eat it with. He tasted it.

"It's good," he said.

She was really pleased.

Suddenly he realised that she'd made the strudel-thingy because it was difficult. When she was concentrating on it she wouldn't think about what he was doing in her garden. So why had she let him, if she hadn't really wanted to? So he wouldn't start crying?

That made him feel ashamed and he didn't want to think about crying. He looked round at the room. There were lots of books, and pictures on the wall. He saw some browny photographs of people from a long while back.

"Who are they?" he asked, pointing at them.

"That's my father and mother when they got married," she said. "And that's my mother with my younger sister and me."

"In Germany?" he asked.

"Yes. In Silesia. It's not Germany now. It belongs to Poland."

He asked, "Where does your sister live?"

"Nowhere," she said. "She's dead."

He didn't know what to say. But she was old, and she just started talking, like old people did.

"We lived in a place called Hirschberg," she said. "After the war, the Allies gave Silesia to Poland, so we had to leave. They loaded us on to a train-truck to go to Cologne. It was January, bitter cold, and we had nothing to eat or drink and there was only room for us to stand. I don't know how long it took. It seemed as if we'd never arrive, but when we got to Cologne a lot of the people in the truck were dead. My mother and my sister were dead."

He went to look at the picture of her and her sister. The sister was a pretty little toddler, and there she was herself, with her hair in two pigtails. Smiling. Happy, because she'd had no idea what was going to happen to her. He'd been like that once.

He asked, "What happened to you after that?"

"My father and I lived in a camp for a long time."

Jusuf had lived in a camp too. He said, "Didn't you hate the people who did that to you?"

She said, "Our people did just as bad things to the Polish people and the Jews." There was a grey, sad note in her voice. He thought, there's a place in her mind where she's really lonely and she's got nowhere to go.

All at once he was saying, "Everything's wrong. I need Mum and Dad and everyone before it can come right. And I haven't got them."

"You can remember them," she said. "I remember my mother and my sister. I remember the good things. I don't want to hate people. I've seen enough hate in my life. It makes me tired."

He said, "Remembering – what good does that do? It doesn't bring people back."

She opened her mouth to say something but he interrupted.

"I want to go now. Please."

She let him.

He went out of the gate and back to his house. He didn't know what to do with himself because suddenly it felt as if all those memories were calling to him to let them in. And he knew if he opened the door, he'd have to admit to himself that everything was gone. His home, and Mum and Dad and Florjan and Granny and Grandad and Uncle Bujar and Ibrahim and Dren.

Vjoleta came downstairs. "You're back," she said.

"She was pleased with me," he said, defiantly.

"She made a – a cherry strudel and we ate it together. I like her now." And then, suddenly, he was saying, "Do you remember how we used to have spitting competitions with cherry stones at home, when we were kids?"

She didn't answer for a moment, then she said, "You swallowed a stone once and you said you'd have a cherry tree growing out of your middle. You weren't scared, you thought it was a great idea. Do you remember that?"

He started to laugh, and then suddenly they were both crying and crying and they went into each other's arms and hugged each other.

Writing to the President
by Kathleen McCreery

The Zimbabwe I fell in love with when I first worked there in 1989 was a young, optimistic nation. Sadly, a corrupt and oppressive government has forced many people to flee. I wrote this story to show how painful it is to be uprooted, and then to seek shelter and face hostility and racism. But presidents and prime ministers don't last forever and popular pressure can make them change their policies. One day Zimbabwe's children will be able to return.

Writing to the President *has been inspired by and is dedicated to the late Yvonne Vera, a great Zimbabwean writer.*

I am writing a letter. I am writing to the President, Mr Robert Mugabe.

In school I learned that my address goes in the top right hand corner and is followed by the date. I write carefully: 10 Bowood Road, Harare, August 12, 2001. August 12 is Heroes' Day in Zimbabwe, when we remember the people who suffered and gave their lives so we could be free.

Once Robert Mugabe was a hero. But that was a long time ago, before I was born. I am 9 years old. And I am very angry with the President. There is a lot I want to say to him.

"When you write a letter," our teacher told us, "you should go straight to the point." So I do.

Dear President Mugabe,

Why did you let them bomb the office where my father works? It was a newspaper office, a peaceful place. People sat at their desks and they looked at their computer screens and they typed, they talked on the telephone and they went to meetings. They were just putting words on paper, as I am now. Is that a crime?

This is not the first time my father's newspaper has been attacked. In January, there was a big explosion and the printing presses were destroyed. And before that people were beaten just for buying a copy. You had to be brave to read the Daily News, and even more brave to work there.

Once I was in town with my mother buying school shoes. I saw the police arresting a man who was selling the paper. They said he was blocking the traffic. The man was not in the way at all. A bus had broken down, but that was not his fault, it happens all the time.

They arrested the newspaper seller, but they have not arrested anybody for bombing my father's office or blowing up the printing presses. And yet everybody knows who has done these things. A Minister in your government, Mr Moyo, said the

Daily News was a threat and should be silenced, and it was.

My father was not in the office when they bombed it, so he was not hurt.

That is not true. I rub out the word 'hurt' and then I write:

...so he was not injured. But he has changed. My father is a big man, with a big smile and a big laugh. He does not laugh anymore. There used to be a light in his eyes, but now it is as though someone has closed a door and shut out the light. He used to clear his plate, but now he pushes it away with food still on it. I think his belly is getting smaller.

He was talking to my mother, the television was on, so they thought I would not hear, but I caught the word 'jail'. And now my father does not spend the night at home any more. He comes without warning for an hour or two and then he goes away again.

My mother has been crying. When our maid Violet dropped a plate on the floor and it smashed, she screamed, and she shouted at Violet. And then she burst into tears. Violet put her arms around my mother and helped her sit down and told me to make some tea. So you see, my mother has enough to worry about already.

I have never written such a long letter. My hand is tired. I wonder if I should tell the President about my Aunty Chido. We went to Gweru for her funeral. Chido was an instructor at the Gweru Teachers' College, and her husband was in the army there. He died ... then it was Chido's turn. My mother was very sad. She said she did not expect to bury her baby sister. When we returned to Harare, we brought my cousins back with us. So now my mother and Violet have five children to care for, and my sister and I have to share our rooms, our clothes, our books and our toys.

My mother is worried about Chido's baby Blessing. If he has AIDS like his mother, he will need special drugs. They are very expensive. My mother works at the Avenues Clinic, but she can't just help herself to the medicine.

She is a radiologist. She takes pictures of people's insides. When she comes home she is always tired. She has to take a lot of pictures of the patients' lungs, because when you have AIDS, you often get TB or pneumonia, and there are more and more people with AIDS in Zimbabwe. One night my mother cried and said she just couldn't do it any more. But she did. She got up the next morning and went to the clinic.

My mother also takes pictures of people's bones. Many people come to the clinic with broken arms and legs and injuries to their heads. HIV-AIDS is not the fault of Robert Mugabe. But the broken bones *are* his fault.

My hand is rested now. So I write,

My mother says the police and army and war veterans are beating everyone, even old women who have nothing to do with the strikes or the protests. People are afraid. And they are hungry. When we go to the supermarket the shelves are bare. Violet and my mother and my cousin Victoria have to queue for hours to buy mealie meal or cooking oil. There is no milk for my small sister or my baby cousin.

I need to get more paper. I go to my father's desk in the room he uses as an office. It has always been messy, but today it is very tidy. It is easy to find the paper and an envelope.

When I come back, my cousin Victoria is sitting on the bed. She is reading my letter. She has a strange look on her face. My cousin is older and bigger than I am. She is 14. Maybe I have spelled some words wrong.

"What is this?" Victoria sounds angry.

"I am sending a letter to the President to…"

Victoria does not let me finish. She slaps me again and again and she yells, "Are you crazy? Are you stupid? Aren't our parents in enough trouble?"

"They are my parents, not yours!" I cry. I am immediately ashamed of myself. We are Shona people, our cousins are our brothers and sisters, there is no difference. And Victoria's parents are dead. But she did not have to slap me.

"And this is how you thank them, you betray them!"

"I thought if I wrote to President Mugabe I could make him understand."

"Why should he listen to a little girl?"

"He has children too, I thought he might..." My voice trails away.

"He doesn't care about other people's children. Now you must promise never to write such a letter again. It is dangerous. Promise!" Her voice is low now, like a hissing snake.

"I promise."

Victoria folds my letter up very small and she puts it in her shoe.

I go outside to the garden and sit underneath the avocado tree. Our old dog, Friday, comes and settles down next to me. He always knows when I am sad. He whines and licks my leg. I scratch him behind the ears. It is chilly in the garden, but I don't move.

In my head there is a cliff and I am walking towards the edge with my eyes wide open, but I can't see that it is a cliff and then Victoria grabs hold of my dress and pulls me back just in time, just before I step into the air. I look down then, and I can see the rocks and my breath leaves my body.

And I turn around and I see my mother and my father and Violet and Blessing and my sister Nokthula and my cousin Tendai and a lot of other people, thousands of people, and the army and police and the Green Bombers and the war veterans are pushing us towards the edge of the cliff, and there is nothing any of us can do.

I am still sitting under the tree when my mother comes out of the house. She is carrying my sweater. She sits on the ground beside me even though she is still wearing her uniform. In her hand she has my letter. It is creased and crumpled now. My mother puts my sweater around my shoulders. She leaves her arm around me. I start to cry.

"I'm sorry, Mother, I thought I could help."

She hugs me and says, "It is an excellent letter, Tsitsi. I am proud of you. You are your father's daughter."

A wave of relief washes over me. "You are not angry with me."

"No. But it is good you did not send the letter. It is also good that I know what you are feeling."

She takes a box of matches from her pocket, and she gives me the letter. I tear it into strips and then we burn each strip on the bare patch of ground under the avocado tree. I watch the fire eat my words and turn them into ash.

❖ ❖ ❖

My mother calls to me from the veranda of our friends' house in Johannesburg, South Africa. I drop my stick and turn. She is smiling, a big broad smile. I run to her.

"We are going, Tsitsi," she says. "We are leaving for London early tomorrow morning. We must get packed. Come and help me."

For a moment I stand rooted to the spot. Then I hurry inside. My mother has put our suitcases on the bed. I help her roll up the mattress Nokthula and I have been sleeping on. Tomorrow morning I will do this for the last time.

It is hard with all four of us living in one room. My father shouts in his sleep. Once he got out of bed and opened the door and was outside before he woke up and realised where he was. He stepped on Nokthula's hand in his rush to get out and she woke up and started to cry. Nokthula went back to sleep, but it took me a long time. I was very tired the next day.

I take my clothes from the bottom drawer in the chest. I wonder where we will sleep tomorrow night. I don't dare hope I will have a room all to myself again, but maybe Nokthula and I will get to share.

I know I should not think like this. My father has suffered a lot. It is not his fault he has nightmares. When he was arrested in Harare he was taken to the Central Police Station. They threw him into a room. The walls were smeared with blood and they told him that soon his blood would be on the walls too. Then they tortured him with electricity. When they put the wires on his fingers they said, "This is for all those lies you wrote about the President." They did other things, terrible things that I don't like to think about. When they released him, he had to go to the hospital for a long time.

I take my school uniform from the hanger in the wardrobe. It is blue with a white collar and cuffs and a matching hat and knickers. It is the uniform of North Park School in Harare and it was new six months ago. I have hardly worn it. I am 10 now and growing tall. The skirt is several inches above my knees.

My mother says, "You don't need to pack that, Tsitsi. In some schools in Britain the children don't wear uniforms. Anyway, they are sure to be different from Harare."

"What shall I do with it?"

"Put it back on the hanger. Beatrice will send home the things we don't take. They will be useful to someone."

"But not to us."

My mother does not react. I don't know whether I have said it out loud or in my head. There are a lot of words piling up behind my lips. I clench my teeth to stop them escaping while I help my mother pack. I want to say that we should put my school uniform away for Nokthula. She always gets my cast-offs. She has started to complain about it. "Why does Tsitsi always get new clothes? I want a new dress too," she whines. So if we aren't saving it for her, it means we are going away for a long time, even longer than we have been living in the spare bedroom of our friends Beatrice and Lovemore Ncube.

And that feels like forever. Because every day is the same as every other day, and I have not been going to school and I miss my friends and my little sister is a pest even though her name means peace. I am bored, and it is not the same doing lessons at home with my mother and sometimes with my father when he has time and does not have a headache, and I am sick of hearing people say how lucky we are to have got out of Zimbabwe.

I know we are lucky that my father was not killed, and they let him go. We are lucky that we had some money and that my father is a respected editor and we have friends in South Africa. And we are very lucky that we could drive across the border in a car instead of swimming across the Limpopo River and being eaten by crocodiles, or trying to get through the barbed wire fence that separates Zimbabwe from South Africa. We are lucky they have not sent us straight back like so many others, or put us in the centre for refugees in Braamfontein where my father says they whip people.

I know all that. But I can't help it. It does not feel lucky to find out that the South Africans do not want us here. My parents went to the refugee office six times to try to get the forms to apply for asylum, and each time they came away empty-handed. It is terrible to wait and wait and still not know what is going to happen.

"Don't put your books in the suitcase, Tsitsi," my mother says. "We'll be in the airplane for 11 hours. You'll need something to read."

I have read the books so often I know them by heart, but I don't say that. I put them on the mattress with my sister's doll. My mother closes the cases and I help her stack them in a corner. Six suitcases. Some bundles and plastic bags. There was no room in the car for anything else.

I go outside to the garden. There is a bare patch where the grass does not grow. The red earth is powdery. It is the dry season. I look at what I have already written with the sharp stick I found.

Violet
Victoria
Tendai
Blessing
Sophia

Violet clapped her hands and cried and cried when we left. "I will never work for another family like this one," she said. My parents tried to help her find another job before they left. They put an advert in the Herald, the government paper: *Maid, excellent references, honest, loyal, good cook, experienced with children, needs live-in appointment.*

But there are a lot of maids looking for work in Harare. The family who are renting our house already had a maid, so Violet has had to go to back to her family in the rural areas. My mother gave her money, clothes and food.

Victoria, Tendai and Blessing have gone to stay with their father's mother. My parents felt very bad about leaving them behind. They have arranged for money from the rental of our house to go to their grandmother. She will need it to pay for their school fees and Blessing's medicine. He is HIV-positive.

Sophia is my best friend. We walked to school together, we played together at break time, we did our homework together. We swam in the pool at her parents' place. We sat side by side in church, and on Saturdays we went to dance and drama classes. I touch the gold chain around my neck, my gift from Sophia.

There is a dog barking in the distance. I pick up the stick and I write 'Friday' in the red dust under the other names. The smell of frying chicken is coming from the house. I remember the peri-peri chicken Violet used to make, and the scones fresh from the oven. I remember sitting between her knees while Violet braided my hair. Her hands were so gentle, not like my mother who was always in a rush.

And I remember Victoria's face as she got into the back seat of the car beside Tendai, and my mother handed Blessing to her. Victoria was 15 years old. I had heard her crying in the night, but in the morning when they left her eyes were dry. She looked as though there was nothing more anyone could do to her.

Underneath the names I write "Goodbye". Then I kick off my sandals and run back and forth as fast as a guinea fowl scattering the dust with my bare feet, leaping and whirling and stamping and dancing and flapping my arms until the letters I have scratched in the red earth of Africa have disappeared.

◇ ◇ ◇

It's noisy in the classroom. Mrs Saunders is talking about the Egyptians, but half of 6B are not listening. They're fidgeting and whispering and waiting for the bell to go. When I first came to the UK I couldn't believe it. At home we stood up when the teacher came in, it was "Yes, Sir," "No, Mam". There were 50 children in my class at North Park School. In places like Highfield or Kambuzuma, the poor suburbs of Harare, there might be 70 or 80. And you could hear a pin drop. Not a sound, except the teacher's voice or her chalk squeaking on the blackboard. Respect!

I keep my head down and try to concentrate. I find history interesting. I want to learn and my parents want me to do well. But it's like walking a tightrope. If it's obvious you're clever, people call you a 'swot'. At my first school in London my hand would shoot up when the teacher asked a question. And she looked surprised, and pleased. But after a while I would see her eyes wander as she tried to get someone else to speak, even when they hadn't put their hands up. And I noticed the others were giving me dirty looks. But it was so boring, just sitting there. Because the lessons were easy, especially maths. We were doing harder work when I was in Grade 5 back home. Anyway, now I wait and see if somebody else is raising their hand, before I stick mine up.

I was really happy when they put me straight into Year 6. I had missed so much I was afraid they might make me repeat a year. No way was I going to sit with the little kids. I am 11 and nearly as tall as my mother.

"Miss! Miss!"

It's Michael Walsh. He used to make fun of my accent. He would start by mimicking me, move on to gobbledygook and then make monkey noises.

Which was rich, since he couldn't write a proper English sentence. Anyway, somebody told the teacher. He got sent to the Head's office, and it stopped.

"So Egypt, right, so Egypt's in Africa, right, so is that where SeeSee comes from? Did she like live in a pyramid and ride on a camel and do that funny writing?"

Oh, no. He just can't leave it alone. And he's deliberately pronouncing my name wrong, even though he's heard it a thousand times.

"No, Michael, Tsitsi is from Zimbabwe which is in southern Africa and..."

Thank God for the bell!

Everybody's crowding and shoving and pushing to get out of the class room and go home. In the hall way, I hear Claire Sullivan calling me. We've started messing around together at break times.

"Tsitsi! Wait up."

She catches up with me.

"Hiya. God, that Michael is such a loser. Listen, I was wondering if you wanted to come over to mine later on. Just hang out. Practise our moves."

Claire launches into Beyonce right there in the school yard.

"*Got me looking so crazy right now, our love's Got me looking so crazy right now in love...*"

Claire's like that. Fearless. Doesn't care what anybody thinks.

"I'll have to ask my mum," I tell her.

"Ah, come on. I've got this wicked new nail polish, and when I try to do my right hand I get it everywhere. You can text me if your mum says it's all right."

She writes down her mobile number for me. I haven't got a mobile, but I can use my mum's. I wave goodbye to Claire and I run home on cloud nine.

I burst through the front door, drop my school bag and run into the kitchen.

"Mother! Mother!" I shout. "Can I go over to Claire Sullivan's, she's really nice, Mum, she's one of the most popular girls in school, and..."

My mother and father are sitting at the table in the kitchen. They have The File out, with a letter on top.

"What's happened?" I ask. My voice sounds loud.

"The Home Office has refused us," my father says. "But don't worry, our solicitor has already started the appeal."

"And NASS have said they need this house. We have to move again." My mother's voice is flat. "Come on. We might as well make a start with the packing."

She does not move. I go to my mother and I stand behind her and put my arms around her shoulders and I kiss the top of her head.

The phone rings. And it keeps ringing on into the night. My father and my mother take turns talking, sometimes in English, sometimes in Shona, telling everyone what has happened. I ask if I can use it, and I tap in a message to Claire:

Sorry, Cnt MAk it. Thx NEway. TsiTsi.

◇ ◇ ◇

Claire Sullivan does not give up. She demands to know why I couldn't come to her house. So I tell her. I tell her about President Mugabe and my father's newspaper and Violet and Victoria and the shortages of food and fuel and the torture and AIDS and Blessing and Friday and Sophia and South Africa.

I ask her what my father has to do to prove that he is in danger in Zimbabwe. I ask her how the British can think of sending asylum-seekers back to Zimbabwe. I tell her about the detention centres in this country where people are going on hunger strike. I shout at her as though it's all her fault. But she isn't cross. She has tears in her eyes.

Claire helps me write a petition. It is addressed to the Prime Minister and it asks him not to send us back and demands that the human rights of all asylum-seekers be respected. I think we should call for UN intervention, but Claire says it would get too long.

We collect 2000 signatures. These names will not be set alight. They will not turn to ash or blow away in the wind or be erased like an email or a text message. We will deliver them to Downing Street. Claire says I am fearless. I say I am my father's daughter and my mother's child.

Beans for Tea
by Lucy Henning and Saeda Elmi

Ameena and her family have recently escaped the war in Somalia and fled to Northolt, England. This story tells how they found friends in their new country and began to settle into a different life. It is based on author Saeda Elmi's true life experiences.

I held the letter in my hand and watched my little sister Deeqa make our tea. I didn't need to read its single sentence again. *Go back to wherever you came from.* That's how little these people knew our family. They didn't even know where we should go back to. I put the letter in the kitchen drawer with all the others.

"I heard them shouting at the door and kicking it. I think they go to Fatima's school," said Deeqa, spooning beans on to plates while I called Mum and my other sister, Fatima. None of us were looking forward to the meal. It was beans on toast again. When it wasn't beans on toast, it was tuna fish sandwiches.

We ate in silence, sitting round the table in the kitchen. When I think about it now, it was like being cast away on an island. In her six months at school, only nine-year-old Deeqa had learnt enough English to make friends outside the family.

My English was only good enough to ask what I wanted, and Mum and Fatima didn't seem to have learnt any. So every evening there was just the four of us, four women who were not used to being alone together.

You see, in Somalia we had never been alone. There was always family, family, family. You needed a degree in maths to work out how many of us there were! A man can have more than one wife in Somalia, and Mum's Dad had three. And all three wives had children. So my mum had twenty brothers and sisters and *they* all had children. This was without my dad's people! And they all loved to go visiting. People were always coming and going, gossiping and nagging, laughing and shouting – it was always business and bustle. Our big house in Mogadishu got so full that my dad had to build another storey on top for us all to hide from them!

Now this tiny house in Northolt felt too big for us. Just me, Mum, Deeqa and Fatima. Dad was still in Somalia, looking after the elders who couldn't leave. The rest of our huge, noisy family was scattered all over the world.

I finished my tea and went upstairs to put on my work uniform. I worked in a burger bar in Hounslow. When I came back downstairs they were all watching the television. Deeqa sometimes explained what was happening, but otherwise we all just sat and stared at it.

It was dark outside.

"Don't forget to lock the doors when I'm gone."

Deeqa laughed. "Like I would forget? They hate us here. Why can't we go home?"

She got up to lock the door after me.

"Be careful," she said. Mum and Fatima didn't say anything. They sat side by side, staring at the English soap opera on the television.

"*Nabadgelyo*. Goodbye."

At least that night it was not raining. In Somalia the only difference between the seasons is the rain or an extra cardigan. In England I could not believe how cold it was. I owned a coat for the first time in my life, but I still shivered as I walked to the bus stop; listening, listening in case those people who wrote the letters were behind me.

I could still taste the beans. You may think beans are nice with chips, but if you had beans for tea almost every night for six months you'd change your mind. Mum did the shopping. It was the only time she left the house on her own. When we first arrived in the UK I went with her. Somebody had to translate, and I had learned English at school. We had crossed the road together and gone into the supermarket. We wanted fish, vegetables, and rice. Mum started to pick up the vegetables, squeeze them and put them down. Suddenly, there was a woman standing next to us.

"Can I help you?" She didn't look so pleased

to see us. We were not used to white people, but then, we weren't used to shopping either.

I had stared at her, feeling suddenly shy and confused. I couldn't think of one word. This supermarket was a long way from the hot sleepy English lessons in my Somali classroom. I knew enough to ask the woman how she was, to tell her my name and wish her a pleasant afternoon. But I did not know how to arrange the strange words I had learnt into questions – where would we find the fish? How do you weigh the vegetables? So Mum and I shook our heads, embarrassed.

The woman said something else in English. She seemed annoyed. Mum put down the vegetables and we moved away. So we came home with beans, tuna fish and white bread – the only things we could buy without asking questions.

And that was it. I hadn't been back with Mum since. I was too busy. In the day I learnt English at college, in the evenings I worked at the burger bar. In between I collected Deeqa from school, went to the benefits office, the housing office, the Doctors. Mum was so scared of this new country I had to do everything. But I just didn't have time to go to the supermarket. So Mum made herself go and then she always came back with the same things, tuna, beans and white bread.

Now I realise it was strange that Mum always bought the same thing. I should have done something about it earlier, but I was so tired all the time. I just took the food and ate it, glad it was not refugee camp porridge that I had to queue for in the baking African sun.

That night I was relieved to come out of the dark night into the bright lights inside the burger bar. The streets didn't feel safe. I couldn't help looking at everyone I saw – the bus driver, the passengers, the passers-by. I was thinking, "Did you write the letters? Did you?" I even looked at my boss that way, the people I worked with.

The burger bar smelt of Haram meat. I did not have enough English to serve behind the counter, so I worked frying fish patties. I burnt my hands all the time on the fat, my beautiful soft hands. In Somalia I had lived in one of the biggest houses in Mogadishu. I had servants working for me. I never cooked or touched anything. If I wanted money, I would smile sweetly at my daddy. If I wanted to go out, I would call our chauffeur to drive me. It made me so angry to be here, where I didn't belong. *Go back to whereever you came from*, said the letters. 'Buy me a ticket!' I thought.

When I got home I checked the front and back door and all the windows. Back home, we never locked anything, there were so many people about. In this country, even the windows had keys. I knew Mum, then Fatima would have checked the locks already, but I had to be sure that everything was safe before I went upstairs.

It was like locking ourselves into a prison. Instead of guards stopping us going where we liked, we had fear. Everything in this country was so strange, and we couldn't make people understand us. We couldn't be like we were in Somalia because we weren't in Somalia. So we locked the doors to try and keep the strangeness out.

Even though the house had three bedrooms, we all slept in the same room. We were scared of the other, empty rooms and we needed to be near each other at night. Mum and Fatima slept on the bed, me and Deeqa on a mattress on the floor. We didn't think about what we were doing. The last door I locked was the door to the tiny bedroom, then I climbed into bed with my sister.

◇ ◇ ◇

The next day I was hanging out the washing, when the old lady next door stuck her big white face over the fence. She smiled at me. I smiled back. I was thinking, is it you with the letters? It's you; you want us to go home.

"Hello!" The old lady was shouting so loud. Why did English people shout? She waved her arm at me. She did not look angry so I went to the fence.

"How do you do?" I said.

"You speak English?" said the old lady.

"A little. My English not good." I laugh when I think about the way I spoke then. In Somalia I was going to be a doctor. I used to laugh and joke with my friends. I was top of my class! In this country I was a different person, a stupid person who couldn't say anything properly.

"You have trouble?" said the old lady. She looked at my face. "Trouble with those children?"

I looked at her blankly. She sighed.

"Ernie!" she called back into the house. "Ernie! Come out here and help." Her husband came out.

"How do you do?" I said. What did they want? What had we done? Had Fatima got into a fight with them?

The old man held his hand out flat, made a pen with his other hand and pretended to write. He then pointed to our back door. He shouted very loudly. **"THEY PUT LETTERS, L-E-T-T-E-R-S, THROUGH YOUR DOOR!"**

What? What?

"Wait," said the old lady. She disappeared into the house and came back with a piece of paper. Ernie did his writing thing again. Then he mimed folding the paper up, making his hands into a letterbox so he could push it through.

"We heard the kids. My wife saw them."

The letters! They were talking about the letters. Maybe they were going to say they agreed with the letters, maybe they told the teenagers to write them.

"Bad boys," said Ernie. "We think they should be ashamed."

The old lady nodded. I did not quite know what they were saying. They looked solemn and cross. But not with me. Then I realised. They did not like the letters! I could not believe it. These white people did not agree with the people who wrote the letters! Someone understood us, someone knew what was happening! I felt a little piece of happiness tug at my heart. I smiled carefully at them.

"Get me a pen, Marion," said Ernie.

Marion went into the house.

"You settling in all right?" asked Ernie. I knew it was a question, but I didn't understand. I nodded. Nodding worked in the burger bar. It seemed to work with Ernie. He put his hands in his pockets and looked at the sky.

"I suppose you find this weather different from where you're from." Weather. I knew that word. You heard that word all the time here. I smiled. I actually smiled. I could feel myself doing it.

"Somalia," I said. "Somalia, very hot."

"It's bad there," said Ernie. "We saw it on the news. Bad, bad, bad. I was in our war you know. Just a little kid. Our house was bombed."

I had no idea what he said, but his voice was friendly. He told the story lots of times after that, which is why I know what he said now.

Marion came back with the pen. Ernie unfolded

the piece of paper and wrote some numbers on it. He wrote their names as well.

"Marion." He pointed to his wife. "Ernie." He pointed to himself. He showed me the paper, then made a pretend telephone with his hands. "Ring. Those boys come back, ring us. OK?" He smiled. Marion smiled.

"Ameena." I said, pointing to myself "Ameena."

They smiled again.

"Cheerio!"

"Cheerio!" That was the first new word Marion and Ernie taught me. They turned and went inside. I stood, holding the piece of paper. You will never believe how happy a scrap of paper with some letters and numbers on it could make you feel.

I ran into the house.

"*Hooyo*! *Hooyo*! Mum! Mum!" I ran upstairs to Mum. "Look! *Saxiib*! *Saxiib*! Friends! Friends!" Mum looked at the piece of paper. She shrugged. But I felt so happy. I ran back down to the kitchen and pinned the paper to the wall.

Friends.

Now Deeqa wasn't the only one with friends outside the family. Marion and Ernie were still strange. They were the first white people who had ever really spoken to us. They had paper on the walls in their house and their cat slept on the furniture, but they were so sweet. It felt good to have Ernie around, whistling and smiling. It made me feel like my dad wasn't so far away. Mum was suspicious. She hardly spoke to them, but I loved to drink tasteless English tea with Marion, looking at the photographs of their grandchildren and, most importantly of all, improving my English.

Then one day I came home from the burger bar to find everyone in the kitchen. Fatima, Mum and Deeqa. Something must have happened. Mum and Deeqa were crying and Fatima was red in the face, really angry.

"Dad!" I said. "Dad!" That was the only thing I could think of.

"No, no," said Deeqa.

Fatima yelled, "That's it! I'm going to kill that woman!" Deeqa was trying to calm her down. I thought Fatima had got into another fight at school. She was not doing very well there. She was angry that she couldn't speak much English, and if the other kids laughed at her, she would hit them. I was forever getting called to the school to talk to the teachers, but Fatima wouldn't listen to me – I wasn't Dad, and Mum would sit and cry.

"What did you do?" I yelled at her. "Who did you hit? I told you, keep away from those kids, walk away! We don't want trouble."

"Those kids!" yelled Fatima. "Those kids are nothing! You know what's been happening? You know what they been doing to Mum?"

Mum was crying, crying. Fatima had lost her

temper and was shouting and shouting. The only person who could tell me what was going on was Deeqa.

"I went in the supermarket after school today with Manisha to buy some crisps," she said. "Mum was in there." Deeqa wiped her eyes. "Ameena, they were throwing the food at her. They weren't putting it in the bags like they do for the other people, they were throwing it at her! She was picking up our beans and bread from the floor; they were saying 'Go back where you came from!'"

"Bitches!" shouted Fatima. "Bitches!"

For six months Mum had crossed the road to that supermarket on her own. Six months this had been happening. They would not let her walk round the store. They followed her and scared her. She would just grab what she recognised and take it to the till. Then they would shout at her and throw her food, her change, everything at her. I could not believe it.

We sat for a long time in the kitchen. We did not want to eat the food now. Mum had paid too much for it. She would not look at any of us. I could not think what to do. Four Somali women on their own in a strange hostile country.

Eventually, Fatima calmed down enough to take Mum up to bed. When they were gone, Deeqa touched my arm. I sat down again. Deeqa was a little girl. She was 9. A year ago, in the refugee camp in Harshin, Ethiopia, she had a sticking-out tummy, like the ones you see on the starving children on the telly. Now she was just thin and small.

"I didn't go to help her," she said.

She stared at the floor.

"Manisha said, 'Look at that old woman, look what they doing,' and I said, 'It's disgusting, they should be ashamed,' but Mum hadn't seen me, so me and Manisha went out."

Deeqa's voice was quiet. She seemed old, old, old.

I rubbed my baby sister's back. In Somalia she had sat on my lap in a cattle-truck on our way to the refugee camp. She had stared out through the slats at a ruined country. Once we drove past a river which flowed through a town. Instead of water in the river there were bodies. Men, women, children. Even some soldiers, but mainly women and children. We had both stared, dumbly. In this country they tell children not to look when this kind of thing is on the news. In Somalia, Deeqa had seen it, smelt it, heard it. I wanted my sister to be safe. I felt angry then. This was better than being sad. It made me want to do something. Angry like Fatima would not get me anywhere, but I knew there were other ways of being angry.

The next morning, I did not go to college. I looked up the words I needed in my college books and practised and practised them until I felt confident. Then I crossed the road to the supermarket and asked to speak to the manager.

"He's busy," said the woman at the till, the same woman who had spoken to us on the first day.

"I want to speak to the manager," I said again. Angry was good. If I hadn't been angry I would have run back home.

"Mr Furbisher!" yelled the woman.

A man in a shirt and tie came out from the back of the store. He was clean-shaven, good looking, like a man from the television.

"This person wants to speak to you."

"Why are your people throwing food at my mother?" I asked.

Mr Furbisher looked surprised. I know why. You can bully someone who cannot speak to you, but someone with a voice, someone with a strong, clear voice? Ha!

"Your mother?" was all he said. Some people in the shop stopped to have a look.

"People saw," I said. "Your people throw food at my mother. They rude!"

Then he got angry. I know why. He was wrong. He had been caught. He said, "We have been having difficulties with her. People have been complaining."

"Difficulties?" I didn't understand that word? I could feel my anger starting to wobble. He was using words I could not understand.

"There's nothing I can do. She's a problem. You go to another supermarket. All you do is make trouble here."

I could not believe it. He folded his arms. That other woman stood behind him. I had no one standing behind me, just a bunch of frightened women at home.

"No," I said. "We want food!" My English was giving up. The less English I could use, the more powerful he became. I started to feel tears coming. I hoped I could control them. I started to understand what Mum had been going through.

"Complain to Head Office if you like," he said. "But we don't want you in here again."

There was nothing I could do but leave the shop. I did not understand all the words he had used, so what could I say? I crossed the road crying.

All the way home I was thinking about Deeqa. I had made it worse. Now we had nowhere to get food from. I did not want to go inside, let Deeqa know I had failed. I walked round the side of the house and went into the garden.

I didn't know what to do. My dad was very far away, in Somalia, and we couldn't cope. I felt alone.

I had forgotten about Marion and Ernie.

"Whatever's the matter, duck?" Marion was leaning over the fence. "Everyone's all right, aren't they? Oh my, oh, you've not had bad news have you? Your dad's safe, isn't he?" I went to the fence and she put her hand on my shoulder. I sobbed and sobbed. She just let me cry and made these sad noises, as if I was a little kid like Deeqa. Then I told her the story. Suddenly I felt her change, from soft and kind to hard and cross. Was she cross with me?

"Ernie!" she shouted. "Ernie!"

Ernie came into the garden.

"What?"

Marion told Ernie what had happened.

"The buggers!" he said. "The bloody buggers."

"We should call the police," Marion told him. "You still got that number that nice young policeman gave you?"

The police!

"No trouble, no trouble," I said. In Somalia, the police were bad news. They would come to our house about once a month and arrest my dad, put him prison for a few days, maybe beat him up a bit and then let him out.

"No police," I said. "We just find another shop." But Ernie was angry now and he went inside the house.

"Don't worry, duck," said Marion. "Have you ever met PC Gary?"

I shook my head.

"He's ever so nice. He goes to our grand-kid's school to talk to the children. He came round here when Ernie got his wallet stolen. He's a community police officer."

I did not know what to do. I thought about police in Somalia and I thought about Deeqa, Mum and Fatima.

Ernie came back out of the house.

"Will you be here at two o'clock?" he asked.

I nodded.

"Good," said Ernie. "He'll be round about then."

◇ ◇ ◇

Marion came to meet PC Gary with me. Funny thing about police in this country – they do not carry guns. If PC Gary had carried a gun we would not have let him in. We had seen what men in uniform could do with a gun. Fatima was still angry so we had told her to go out, and Mum was so scared she would not come downstairs. She thought we were making trouble and that the policeman would take her away. This country had made my mum think like a little girl.

I had a big surprise when the policeman came in. Deeqa spoke to him, spoke to a white man, her elder, in front of everybody.

"Hello PC Gary!" She looked really happy, I thought, maybe this isn't so bad then.

"Hello!" the policeman smiled at her.

"You come to my school!" said Deeqa. "Be safe with fireworks!"

PC Gary laughed.

Of course, Marion offered him tea. Even policemen in your country drink tea when something goes wrong. Marion brought tea bags from next door and we all sat and drank English tea.

"So," said PC Gary. "Your mother has suffered racist abuse." These were new words for me. In Somali, we don't think about the colour of your skin so much as the religion you are. Maybe people think Deeqa is prettier than me because her skin is lighter, but that's all. Perhaps my dad protected us too well in Somalia, but I never thought before that the colour of your skin made you different.

PC Gary was looking at me.

"Marion said the people in the supermarket..."

"They rude!" I said. "They not listen to me. They throw food at her!"

PC Gary nodded. I was so cross that I did not know how to explain. I wanted this man to listen to what I had to say and not treat me like the supermarket manager had.

Then Deeqa spoke up.

"I saw them," she said. "I went with my friend, we went in and they were throwing the shopping instead of putting it in the bags like they do for everyone else."

PC Gary wrote this down. Deeqa went on to tell him everything – the letters, the shouting in the night, everything.

My little sister did not learn English in Somalia like me. She had just been at a school in England for six months. I sat and listened to her big English. She even used words I did not understand. In her school they had every colour of the rainbow, Somali, Caribbean, Indian, so how come her English was so good?

"We eat the same food," I said. "We eat beans and white bread and tuna fish because they throw it at her and won't let her look round the shop."

"That should not be happening," PC Gary looked very serious. "It's racist abuse. We have laws about this. I'm sorry it had to happen to your mother. Can I talk to her?"

My mum was angry enough that Deeqa and I were talking to a man. A policeman made it worse. She was angry and scared and upstairs. She wouldn't come down, even when Deeqa asked her to.

"She scared," I explained. "She scared of police, of mans. Our dad is in Somalia. We have no mans to look after us."

"Only Ameena," Deeqa grinned at me. Marion smiled. Deeqa just didn't care, she was so little and she talked to the big policeman like he was a friend.

"That's what's been happening," I said. "I don't know what to do."

Marion touched Deeqa's shoulder. "Show him the letters."

Deeqa went into the kitchen and came back with them. I looked at the pile of letters in her hand. So many!

PC Gary looked through them.

"It's those lads across the road," said Marion. "I've seen them a few times."

PC Gary looked at me. "Can I take them with me?" he asked.

I nodded.

"Thank you."

He stood up. He shook my hand. He shook Deeqa's hand. Thank God Mum did not see that. We got to know him a bit better before we told him he mustn't touch Somali women, but we knew he was just being friendly.

Then he went. We all sat back down.

"There you are," said Marion. "PC Gary will sort it out."

An hour later PC Gary came back.

"Right," he said. He gave us a card with a telephone number on it.

"Any more trouble, you call this number. Tell your mum. If she just says Somali and her phone number, we will find a translator and call her back. Anyone upsets you, or worries you, you let us know."

He put his hat on. Your policemen have weird

hats. As he went to the front door he said, "You've been very brave. Many people put up with this because they're scared. Marion told me how you crossed the road to speak to them. Your mum should be very proud of you."

Then PC Gary was gone. Deeqa and I stood and watched him go down the path. Back home we had watched Superman movies. Christopher Reeve was our favourite Superman: he always made everything all right. PC Gary was like Christopher Reeve.

The next day, Deeqa, Fatima and me took Mum to the shop. The woman was there. I felt Fatima bristle up.

"Good morning," the woman said. Mum did not look up. We took our time going round the shop. We filled our basket up. We had vegetables and fish. No beans. I will never eat beans again. When we got to the check-out the woman packed our bag for us.

She counted Mum's change into her hand. My Mum did not look up, but me and Fatima and Deeqa looked right at her. Now we had people standing behind us. Marion and Ernie and PC Gary.

It was a long time before Mum felt safe going to the supermarket, but they never threw the food at her again. After a bit Mum got so brave, she got on a bus and went to the big supermarket in Hayes.

Deeqa began to bring friends home from school. Slowly, slowly, Fatima started talking to other kids.

I enrolled on a course to be a nursery nurse, looking after children. I wouldn't be a doctor, but I was getting somewhere. All these things didn't happen like magic, they took months and months, years and years. But things got better and better.

At first we had just two phone numbers on our wall, the one PC Gary had given us and Marion and Ernie's. Later on, we added others; Deeqa's friend Manisha, the people from my course, Fatima's school friends. I liked to add more numbers, more links to the people in our new country. For a long time we didn't buy an address book because we liked to remind ourselves every day how things were changing.

Somalia will always be a long way from England and we will always talk for hours about its mountains and cities, about our family that is now spread all over the world in all the countries that would take them. But we have learnt to live in your country that used to be so strange to us. I even like to be here now, visiting people, going shopping, going to college. This country even seems warmer to me now that I have friends.

A Place to Hide
by Rob Porteous

Mukhtar comes from a village in Darfur in western Sudan, close to the mountains knowns as the Jebel Marra. In recent years there have been many conflicts in the area between villagers and the Arab Janjaweed militia. Many people have been displaced and their villages destroyed.

A stray plastic bag scurried along the pavement, past a black-haired boy in jeans and a T-shirt, crouching at the entrance to the station. A motorbike roared by. The boy felt the heat of the exhaust on his face, caught the smell of petrol in the air, and tensed, pressing his back against the stone arch. In his mind he smelled the petrol thrown from a can, heard the crackle and spit as the house burned.

"*Ashur bel bard.* I'm cold, Mukhtar."

Mukhtar glanced down at the smaller boy at his side. "*Laa tukhaf.* Don't be frightened, Abdi." He put his arm protectively round his brother. "I'll look after you. Mama said she wouldn't be long."

They huddled together in the wind. Abdi played with the tag on their battered suitcase, while Mukhtar scanned the people in the square. Beyond the bus stand, he saw his mama coming towards them, carrying a bag of shopping. Snatching Abdi's hand he ran across the road. A car horn blared. Then he was rubbing his head against the folds of her dress, smelling the familiar tang of her body.

"*Kwaïs*, OK. Don't fuss now, Mukhtar." She stroked his head. "I'm here. It's over now. We'll be all right." She knelt to take his face between her hands. "This is Mohammed. He's going to help us."

Mukhtar looked up to see a thin-boned man grinning down at him. He smelled the cigarette smoke on his clothes and the cheap aftershave as he bent his face towards him. "*Jaïd*, Mukhtar, what do you think?" he asked. "I bet you'll grow up to be a fighter like your dad."

Mukhtar twisted away from the hand that touched his shoulder.

Mohammed held his hand up. "Come. I was only joking." He led them across to a battered Ford car, parked on the far side of the square. The engine spluttered into life.

As Mohammed drove through the darkening streets, Mukhtar yawned sleepily. Another move. Another town. A drone of traffic accompanied their journey from place to place. London. Newcastle. Birmingham. And now Liverpool. The buildings merged into a blur of rain-soaked walls.

Pigeon droppings littered the front yard of the house. Mohammed unlocked the door and ushered them in. The rooms smelled damp. In a corner someone had pulled the paper from the wall. A ragged chair and a sofa seemed lost in the empty space.

"*Haza al bayit*," Mohammed explained. "This is the house. Upstairs there are bedrooms. You won't be disturbed."

"Good. But does no one live here?"

"It is NASS house."

"So," the woman shrugged. "You'll come tomorrow?"

Mohammed nodded. "Good night." He disappeared into the hall. As he opened the front door to the gathering dusk, the squawks of seagulls entered the house. The door banged shut behind him.

Silently, Mukhtar watched his mother prepare food in the small kitchen, hearing the click of the knife as she chopped vegetables and the flare of the gas as she set the rice to boil. Abdi was already asleep, curled up on the sofa. Mukhtar stood up and walked into the front room, where a single bed, with a crumpled duvet, faced the bay window.

"I'll sleep downstairs," he informed his mother when he came back to the kitchen.

"If you like. Eat now, the food is ready." The hiss of the gas stilled.

❖ ❖ ❖

Turning away from the dawn light Mukhtar curled into the warm hollow of the bed. In the distance a bell jingled. A herd of goats were scavenging the sandy hillside surrounding his village. In a moment he would get up and fetch water from the well. Balancing the pole on his shoulder so that no drop spilled on the dry earth, he'd watch the rising sun gild the dome of the mosque. By the time he got back, his father would be lacing up his boots, preparing for a day in the fields.

A car passed, blaring music. Accompanied by a chatter of foreign words, footsteps approached and receded. Mukhtar pushed his head deeper into the pillow. He could no longer see the fields surrounding his village.

"Mukhtar."

Reluctantly, he opened his eyes. Abdi was standing at the side of the bed. "What do you want?"

"Where's Papa?"

"They took him away."

"Who?"

"The bad men."

"When's he coming back?"

"He's not coming back."

"I don't like it here," Abdi cried. "I want Papa."

Mukhtar watched his brother's face crumple and his chest collapse into sobs. "Listen," he said.

"They killed him. The big men with the clubs."

He grabbed Abdi's arm, just as he had done when he first heard the shouting. He'd run to the neem tree opposite the house, scrambling up its lower branches, pulling his brother behind him. He'd seen the line of men stroll down the dusty path, their eyes flashing, heard their jeering words, watched them duck under the eaves of their house and through the open doors. Wanting to cry out, he'd held his body rigid in the folds of the tree for a long time.

Feeling tears on his cheek Mukhtar angrily brushed them away. He pulled his brother towards him. "Don't worry. I'll keep you safe. There, now, don't cry."

"Mukhtar!" His mother's voice travelled down the stairs. "What have you done?"

"Nothing."

She was standing in the doorway, a frown on her face. Then she marched across the room, cuffed Mukhtar on the head and drew her younger son towards her. "I told you not to frighten him."

Mukhtar lowered his eyes, staring at a stain on the patterned carpet.

After a moment his mother stretched out her hand to fondle his hair. "Come. Let's make breakfast."

◇ ◇ ◇

Later Mohammed took them all back to the centre of town. In the drizzling rain they waited outside an office with a fair trade poster in the window. Mukhtar kicked a can against the wall till his mother pulled him away. Inside, he heard a babble of voices in different languages. People drifted between desks littered with papers and empty cups. A telephone rang. A man's angry voice rose above the eddy of conversation. Then Mama was seated at a desk and the official asked the familiar questions: *Where do you come from? Why? When did you come? How? Show me your papers. You have two children? Where is your husband now?* He heard his mother's tired voice retelling their story that seemed, with each telling, ever more threadbare.

The man picked up the receiver and spoke briefly, before handing over a set of keys. "For the time being, you can stay where you are."

That afternoon Mukhtar trailed upstairs, where Mama was sorting washing on the bed. "Can I play in the yard?"

"If you like. Mohammed said he would find a school for you tomorrow."

"I don't like him," Mukhtar protested. "We're all right on our own."

"He's a friend," Mama said. "Don't bother me now."

Mukhtar took his ball outside and kicked it

towards the far wall of the garden. The ball sailed in a gentle arc through the space between the wall and the tangled branches above it.

He looked round. No one was watching. He darted to the end of the garden, scrambled over the wall and dropped on to a patch of waste ground, where a muddy track twisted between trees and bushes down to a stream. A boy was standing on the path, clutching his ball. As they eyed each other Mukhtar noticed the boy's tangle of auburn hair above his white, podgy face.

"Give me ball," Mukhtar said, awkwardly.

The boy just stood there.

"My ball..." Mukhtar shifted from one foot to the other.

"Oh, is this yours?" The white boy feigned surprise. Glancing down, he let the ball slip through his fingers. It rolled away into a patch of nettles.

Mukhtar ran forward to scoop up the ball, yelping as he felt the stings on the back of his hands.

The boy laughed.

Mukhtar's face burned. He could hear his mother calling from inside the house. The boy had picked up a stick and was twirling it in his hand. Mukhtar hesitated, then ran back and scrambled over the wall.

The stick hit the branch of a tree behind him. He dropped the ball in the corner of the yard and tried to slip unnoticed into the house.

Mama had her back to him, but whipped round as she heard his tread on the steps. "Where've you been? Don't you go straying out of my sight, d'you hear?"

◇◇◇

Mukhtar's hands still itched as he leafed through a magazine that evening. His heart beat too fast. The white boy was stupid, but he might be dangerous. He'd have to keep an eye on him if he was going to protect the family.

"What's the matter?" Mama finished the dishes and dried her hands on a towel.

"Nothing." He hunched down in the armchair, letting the magazine drop on the floor.

Hearing Mohammed's knock, Abdi scampered into the hall to meet him.

"I've seen the head teacher of Hannah Road School," Mohammed said when Mama had made tea and the two of them had settled on the sofa. "An Indian lady. I have a form to take back." He took a folded paper from his pocket.

"I don't want school." Mukhtar stared into Mama's eyes. "I want to stay with you."

"You need to learn," said Mama, squinting at the form. "What do they want?"

"Information." Mohammed took out a pen, read out the questions and scribbled down the answers.

Mukhtar saw how close they sat, almost touching, how Mama curled her right foot under her body, settling back into the cushions and letting the shawl slip off her head when she smiled at Mohammed's jokes. Mukhtar closed his right eye, trying to block out the man who shouldn't be there.

"So. It's finished." Mohammed put his arm round Mama's shoulders. "Tell me what you did today, Mukhtar."

"Nothing."

Mohammed laughed. "That way, you'll never get a nice car or a wife when you grow up."

"I don't care."

◇ ◇ ◇

Mukhtar slept fitfully that night. Moaning, he scratched the backs of his hands where they still hurt from the nettle stings. Then, as rain spattered against the windowpane, he stirred, pulling the bedcover more tightly against the night. Tyres squelched on the surface of the road. Water splashed from the broken gutter. No one cared. Back home the rains that came after the long heat were treasured. A water butt outside each house gathered the precious drops as they fell, glistening, from a clouded sky. As a young child Mukhtar would run out, opening his hands to catch them.

But the bad men would come to knock over

the barrels, jeering as the water drained away. Then they would beat whoever they found.

Mukhtar screamed.

"There, there, it's just a dream." His mother was bending over him, her hand on his cheek.

"Mama, when the bad men come, where will we hide?"

"Don't worry, little one." She stroked his head. "This is England. The bad men will not come for us here."

"But Mama, what if they do?" He grabbed her arm. "We need a place to hide."

"Silly boy," she smiled, "we're safe now."

But Mukhtar saw the fear at the back of her eyes. He wondered again why adults lied.

◇ ◇ ◇

At breakfast, Abdi didn't eat much and played with the slice of bread on his plate till it fell, butter side up, on to the floor.

Mukhtar stared out of the glass door into the garden. It was too small to hide them, the trees too stunted, to offer shelter. But beyond, over the back wall, the waste ground was more promising, with taller trees and thick bushes along the stream. As soon as he could, he'd explore it further.

His chance came when Mama had finished the washing-up. "I'm going to the shop," she said.

"D'you want to come?"

"No." Seeing her frown, he added, "I'll be all right," and picked up the magazine he'd discarded yesterday.

When the front door clicked behind them, he darted into the garden. This time the waste ground was deserted. He heard the ripple of water over stone. Walking upstream, he noticed the trees were too tall and spread out to make good hiding places. The bushes were better.

The open space ended in a high wall, where water gurgled from a grubby pipe. Retracing his steps, Mukhtar tensed as he saw the white boy waiting for him at the edge of the stream.

"It's you again." The boy grimaced. "Where d'you come from?"

"Birmingham."

"No, I mean, really?"

"Sudan."

"Where's that?"

"Africa."

"Oh," He stared at the other boy. "You're not one of them asylum-seekers my grandad's on about, are you? He says you should go back home."

"Here is home now," Mukhtar said.

"Not if we don't want you." The boy picked up a stone and tossed it over his shoulder. "Sorry," he said, laughing as it struck Mukhtar on the arm.

Mukhtar stepped forward. "Don't!"

The next moment they were grappling together. The white boy hit Mukhtar in the chest. Panting, Mukhtar twisted the boy's arm behind his back. The boy shoved backwards, pushing Mukhar on to the ground. Stones dug into Mukhtar's back as he fought the boy off. Struggling together, they rolled towards the stream.

A bird swooped down to the water, sending up a flurry of spray that soaked their T-shirts. The white boy laughed. After a moment, Mukhtar joined in. "Let's call it quits." The white boy stood up. "What's your name?"

"Mukhtar."

"Mine's Tom. I'm staying with my nan at the moment." He waved towards the houses on the other side of the stream. "Just till my mum gets better."

Mukhtar shifted from one foot to the other. "I must go...."

"D'you want to see my den?" Tom interrupted. "It's over there, at the bottom of Nan's garden." Without waiting for an answer, he stepped from stone to stone across the stream. "Mind yourself," he warned from the other side, "or you'll get stung again." He lifted aside a framework of twigs and leaves to reveal an opening at the base of a bush. "These rhododendrons have bags of room inside."

Mukhtar peered into the greenish shade. The dark branches made a tent-like awning over his head. The floor was swept clean, with a square of carpet in the centre.

"I got that from under the stairs," Tom explained, " and sneaked it down here when Nan wasn't looking."

"It's fine place," said Mukhtar.

"D'you think so?" Tom looked up, pleased.

For a moment they stood there, saying nothing.

"Sorry," Mukhtar said. "Now, I must go."

"Why don't you come round to play this afternoon?" Tom asked.

Mukhtar shook his head. "I must look after my brother, for Mama."

"At the weekend, then."

"Maybe," said Mukhtar, and he turned and scurried back across the stream. Luckily Mama had not yet returned. He was able to throw himself into the armchair before he heard the key turn in the lock.

"You'd never believe how long the queue was," Mama grumbled.

Thinking about the den, Mukhtar relaxed a little. It was a good hiding place. You could make an escape route through the tangle of creepers along the stream. The trouble was Tom had made it. He wasn't sure he could trust him.

That evening, Abdi was in a bad mood. A wheel had come off his toy police car. He brought it to Mukhtar. "I want you to fix it."

"The rod's bent. And there's a bit missing."

"Fix it."

"I can't."

Abdi threw the car away.

"Stop squabbling and come and eat." Mama put the rice and chicken on the table.

"I met a boy called Tom," Mukhtar said. "He lives round here. He's invited me round to play.

His mother clicked her tongue. "Don't get friendly with English boys. You don't know what they're like."

"You're friends with Mohammed," Mukhtar protested.

"He can help us." His mother picked the meat from a bone. "He's a full refugee, with papers. He knows what to do." Hearing a knock, she said, "That'll be him. Go and open the door."

Mukhtar dawdled down the hall.

"Hello, young man," Mohammed laughed. "Is your mama in?"

Without answering, Mukhtar stepped aside to let him into the house.

"Mohammed?" Mama called from the room. "Thank goodness." She rose to greet him. "I don't know what to do with them. Abdi's in a mood and already Mukhtar wants to play with the English boys."

"Why not?" Mohammed sat back on the sofa. "There's no harm in that."

◇ ◇ ◇

On Saturday afternoon Tom knocked on the door. "I've come to call for Mukhtar," he said.

"Mukhtar!" Mama called. "What does the boy want?"

"This is Tom," Mukhtar explained. "Can I go out now?"

"Where?"

"To his house. Round the corner."

"I suppose so."

As they walked down the road, Tom explained about his nan. "You've got to wipe your feet on the mat, or she'll be cross. She keeps the house ever so tidy. She makes me scrub my face *every morning*."

Tom's nan's house felt strange, with its plumped up cushions and mantelpiece crowded with china ornaments.

Tom's grandad was sitting in the armchair by the window, reading a paper. As Mukhtar entered he looked up and spluttered over his tea.

"What's that, George?" Nan called from the kitchen.

"Nothing, Mabel." Fussily, he pulled out a handkerchief and blew his nose.

"We're going down to the den," Tom said.

"Suit yerselves," his grandad replied, staring hard at the dark-skinned boy.

Mukhtar felt the stare following him as he and

Tom stepped through the French windows into the garden, where neat rows of flowers guarded the path down to the bushes at the bottom.

Tom stooped through the opening to the den. "Make yourself at home."

"The way your grandad looked," Mukhtar said. "He didn't like me."

"Once he gets to know you he'll be all right." Tom settled himself on the floor. "He just thinks people should stay in their own countries."

Mukhtar glanced away. "I didn't want to come here. I wanted to stay in our village, with my father."

"What does he do?"

"He was farmer."

"Does he live with you?"

"No," Mukhtar muttered. "They killed him."

"Who?"

"The bad men. They are attacking us always. They knocked him down and beat him and took him away."

"Oh." Tom scratched his ear, then picked up a fallen rhododendron leaf and began shredding it in his fingers "My dad's dead too. He was a soldier, in Iraq. One morning someone came to their checkpoint and blew himself up." He threw the shredded leaf away, pulled a piece of paper from his pocket and unfolded it. "Here, look."

Mukhtar saw a picture of a man with a rifle

across his knees. "How old's your dad?"

"Thirty-five. That's his combat uniform. In his last letter he said it was too hot for the desert." Tom folded the picture away. In the silence a blackbird whistled. "Do you want to help me make a way through the brambly bit to those bushes beside the stream?"

The boys fell into a rhythm of working together, tearing off the smaller branches, carefully lifting the bramble shoots aside and clearing the earth floor beneath. As they worked, they said little. Contentedly, Mukhtar listened to the wind in the trees and the plop of waterfowl foraging in the stream.

Tom flopped on to the floor. "Let's stop now."

Mukhtar looked up. "It's late. I have to go."

"See you tomorrow," Tom called as Mukhtar scrambled across the stream.

The house was silent. Neither Mama nor Abdi were in the living room. Two at a time he mounted the stairs. In the back bedroom he heard Abdi talking to himself. Mukhtar pushed open the other door.

"Who's that?" From the bed in the darkened room, he heard Mohammed's voice.

"Mukhtar?" his mama asked. "I thought you

were with your friend."

"Mama? What's going on?"

"Get lost, son," Mohammed growled.

Mukhtar ran back downstairs, slamming the door of his room and wedging the chair against the handle. He ran to the corner, drew his knees under his chest and banged his fist on the mirror propped against the wall. His jaw tightened. His breath came in harsh bursts. He wanted to hurt himself.

"Mukhtar?"

Mama was coming down the stairs, knocking on his door. He banged harder, feeling the cold touch of the glass, its dampness, and the sharp pain as it broke, cutting a red line along the edge of his hand.

Over and over as he lay on the bed, words formed themselves in his mind, an accusation from his father's spirit. "How could you?" Maybe Papa was still alive. Maybe he had escaped to live in the forest, hunted like an animal, waiting for the day when Mukhtar would come, riding on his camel across the desert, to rescue him. Together they would travel from place to place, trading precious stones in the shuk or living off the imam's bounty, drinking at the fountain in the mosque courtyard, and finding shelter at some rich merchant's door.

Under the sticking plaster, the side of his hand

throbbed. He turned over, drifting back into sleep. Together he and his papa would come to the Three Towns and travel down the Nile before crossing the mountains to Port Sudan, where they would board a dhow to sail the Arabian Sea.

He watched dawn break over the dark waters. The screech of gulls following the boat mingled with the slap of waves against the wooden hull.

◇ ◇ ◇

"Open up!" Someone was shouting, hammering with his fist on wood. The bad men had returned! Mukhtar slid under the bed, pulling the duvet down so that only a spy hole remained between it and the floor. The smell of dust stuck in his nostrils. Lying lizard-still in the dark, he choked back a cough.

"Open up!" In a moment the lock on the door would give way and the men would burst in to ransack the house. His only chance was to grab Abdi, and run to the neem tree where they could hide. But if the men caught him in the hall, he would die. Better to lie still, wait for the first attack to pass.

"Police! Open up!" Mukhtar tensed as he heard footsteps come down the stairs. His mother, dressed only in her shift, crossed his line of sight. He heard the front door swing back. Big men with heavy boots stampeded past her, up the stairs. One man came into the front room. From under the bed Mukhtar could see his boots pressing into the carpet. Another man had hold of Mama's arm. A gun bulged in the holster at his hip. "What is your name?" he barked.

"Mrs Bagogo."

"Who else lives here?"

"My children."

"Their names?"

"Mukhtar and Abdi."

"And their father?"

"He is not here. I am alone."

Under the bed, Mukhtar's thoughts raced. The bad men had come for him, just as they had come for his father. His only hope was to run away.

"Take charge of Mrs Bagogo, will you?" the gunman ordered the man in the front room. "Tell her to get her papers, and to put some clothes on, for God's sake!" He marched into the street, where Mukhtar heard him speaking on his phone.

"Now then, missus, can you show me the letter from the Home Office?" The polished boots moved away.

Now was his chance. Abdi would have to fend for himself. He scrambled up, darted through the living room, down the steps to the garden, and lunged for the back wall, expecting at any moment to feel the bullet of a gun. A piece of loose plaster came away in his hand. Then he was over, running down the path to the stream and splashing through the water to the shelter of the bushes. In a single movement, he pushed aside the framework of twigs, crawled through, and fitted it back into place. Then he collapsed, gasping, in the far corner of the den.

In the darkness, Mukhtar saw again the deserted path outside his house on that last evening in the village. The shouting had stopped. A breeze ruffled the leaves of the neem tree. He saw again his father's shadow swaying ahead of him as he returned from the fields. He wanted to call out but no sound came. Steadily Papa drew nearer to the edge of the yard. Then the bad men spilled out of the house through the broken door and beat him into the dust. Blood trickled from his mouth. Like a crushed insect he lay there, till they dragged him away. Then the house caught fire. Mukhtar smelled petrol in the air.

At the sound of someone approaching the den he jerked awake. He froze, not breathing, trying to blend into the background of twigs and leaves.

Tom stooped through the entrance. "Hey! What you doing here? I know I said you could come and play, but this is *my* den."

Mukhtar held his finger to his lips. "The bad men come," he whispered. "I am hiding."

"What bad men?"

"With guns. Into the house."

"But they can't. You ought to tell the police."

"They *are* police."

"I don't get it." Tom frowned. "Look, if this is a game..."

"Not game," said Mukhtar. "They kill my papa, now they come for me."

Tom stared at him. "You really believe it, don't you?"

Mukhtar nodded.

Tom looked away. "When they told me my dad had died, I didn't believe it. I thought it was just a story. It was like I had this stone in my belly. I kept trying to push it away but it wouldn't budge. Grandad wanted to shoot all the terrorists, but I just wanted my dad back." He looked at Mukhtar. "When Dad was home, he'd sit on the edge of my bed and tell me stories of all the places he'd seen."

"When my papa came from the fields, he told the stories of our tribe, before the bad men came." Mukhtar sighed. "That was good time."

For a while, as the morning woke up around them, they sat together.

"Listen," Tom said at last. "If you're going to hide here you're going to need some food. I'll see what I can sneak out without Nan seeing."

"No!" Mukhtar protested, but Tom was already making his way back up the path.

Left alone, Mukhtar felt tired. He heard the whir of a bird's wings, the babble of the stream over the stones. All he wanted to do was sleep.

◇ ◇ ◇

He woke to the sound of Mama's voice, calling to him from a long way off. She was running down the path, pushing aside the framework of twigs, hugging him, holding his head against her breast. "My boy, my boy, why did you run away?"

"The bad men came for me," Mukhtar said. "This is my place to hide, Mama."

"Oh son, don't you understand?" As she rocked back and forth against the bush's stem her tears wet his face. "It was Mohammed they came for. Not you."

"Mohammed?"

"He lied to me, as men do. He has no papers. He should not be here. They came to take him away." She sighed. "I thought he could help us, but... he was just the same as the others." She kissed his cheek. "You were right not to trust him."

"Will we be safe here, Mama?"

"Who knows?" She stroked his head. "But it's not your job to protect us, son."

Mukhtar let his head rest on her body. He was so tired of waiting for the next attack.

Outside the den, he heard Tom's footsteps.

"Excuse me," Tom said. "Nan says you're both to come in for a cup of tea." Tom smiled at Mukhtar. "We'll keep each other company."

Shyly, Mukhtar smiled back.

The Final Border
by Lily Hyde

*Every year thousands of migrants from Africa and
Asia move through the countries of Eastern Europe
and the former Soviet Union on their way to the West.
For the people-smugglers, it's just a question of
finding the easiest border to cross. For the migrants in
this story, it's yet another stage in a long journey to
escape a civil war in Sudan. The final stage – or so
they think...*

When the back of the truck swung open, snow was
coming down. Twirling white spots and streaks on
a dark grey sky, like the fuzz on the TV screens
when the government shut down the broadcasts,
but this was soundless. The people stared in dazed
astonishment, and the boy shouted out, a word
from a country where it never snowed.

Adam clapped his hands over his mouth, so that
all that could be seen were his wide shocked black
eyes. Shouting was something you weren't supposed
to do. He waited, shoulders hunched, for his uncle's
hand to descend.

"You fool! Don't you know..."

"Yes, I know."

But all the same, snow! It was such a shock,

196

coming out of the cramped darkness of the truck into this spinning white world. All the same, he couldn't help grinning.

The driver was already stacking the crates again before closing up the back of the truck. "That house. You go now, quick."

"What's there? Who will we meet? How far to the border?" Uncle Abakar looked impatiently at Adam to translate. Adam was the only one who could speak English, apart from Awa, whose English, as far as Adam could tell, was as perfect as her smooth black skin. But Awa hardly ever said anything. *Except to me.*

"You wait for night. Walk with guide." The man made walking movements with two fingers across his palm. "Four, five kilometre. And then..." He opened both hands wide in a starburst, grinning.

"Then what?" *We explode? We get fried on an electric fence?*

"Then border. You over. Where you want to be."

Kalif was agitated, twitching like all his strings were stretched too tight. "But you were going to take us right to the border. That was our agreement."

"How do we know they're waiting for us? Ask him, Adam."

The driver climbed back into the cab and waved a mobile phone out of the window. "I call. You go. Everyone happy." He was in such a good mood now he was getting rid of them. Now he had their money, he even started to sing.

"*You should be so happy, happy happy happy, you should be so happy in lo-o-ve!*"

"*Lucky*," said Awa quietly. "The word is *lucky*."

"That also."

The headlights flicked on, illuminating the dancing whiteness in the air. The truck reversed and drove away, leaving them in snowy silence.

The road was perfectly white, perfectly smooth. A little further on the village began – not even a village, just a few small low houses under fat hats of snow. A dog barked, and some windows glowed dimly yellow, but otherwise the place looked deserted.

"Look at the prints we leave in this snow stuff," Ghazi commented, treading round in a circle and admiring the result. Amongst themselves they spoke Arabic, a language they all shared, although they were from different tribes and even countries. "It's worse than wet sand."

Kalif fussed. "We agreed they would take us to meet the guides. That's what we paid for."

Adam wondered how long Kalif had been on the road. He was like Uncle Abakar; he never learned. Adam had learned long ago that expecting proper plans and arrangements, expecting answers to questions was a waste of time. On this particular road (east to west, south to north) you handed over your money and crossed your fingers. People-smugglers never stuck exactly to their promises but if you complained, you got nowhere – you were off the road for good.

"C'mon, chill." Ghazi slapped Kalif cheerfully on the shoulder. "We're nearly there."

"And it's snowing!" said Adam. "It's like pictures of Austria, it's like…"

"You talk too much," his uncle grunted. "She has the right idea."

He meant Awa. She had walked away up the road, her small upright figure fading into the falling snow. Silenced, they set out after her.

Adam's uncle's words smarted. It was Adam who had brought them this far, just a few kilometres from the border, and still Abakar could do nothing but criticise. Adam took refuge inside his head.

Hi, Jad. You won't believe where we are now. Ninth, tenth country… Can't remember. Not important. What's important is that it's the last one. This is the Final Border. The next letter I write you is going be a real one. I'm going to send it from Austria. I'm going to be drinking Viennese coffee, and staring up at all those big banks, and getting to be a banker myself, never mind cousin Ahmed's fruit and veg stall. I'll send back money so you can come over and rescue me from the Hand.

He called Abakar 'the Hand' because he saw the back of it so often. If his uncle wasn't slapping him to be quiet, to be serious, he was holding it up importantly to make a speech, as if he thought he was still a big-shot army boss. He was the only close family Adam had left, and sometimes Adam hated him.

Outside the house the driver had pointed at a little figure made out of snow. The body was a roundish lump, the head a second smaller one. It had a row of buttons made of fir cones, holes for eyes, a smile of potato peelings. A branch with splayed twigs at the end made one outstretched hand. It was funny and a bit sinister.

"You like my snowman?" A small boy was looking at them from the doorway. "I wait for you. When dark, I take you to border. What your name?"

Adam was instantly suspicious. But it was only a boy, after all. "Adam."

"I'm Sasha."

"Stupid boy!" Abakar snapped. "What is he saying? What did you tell him? Is he waiting for us?"

"Yes," Adam said sullenly.

"Is he's going to take us to the border? When?"

"*You* ask him."

And up comes the Hand. *O, Jad, I'm so tired of this.*

"After border, where you go?" said Sasha.

"Why you asking?" replied Adam. Sasha was just a kid. He didn't even know that you never asked questions on the south-north, east-west road. "The other side."

"Where you from? How you get this far?"

Adam turned away from the boy's gap-toothed, inquisitive face. You should never tell anyone how you got here. There were only two phrases he needed to know: "I am seeking asylum" and "They will kill me if I go back".

Something cold and wet hit his right ear. He spun round and got the next ball of snow in his chest. The boy giggled.

Uncertainly Adam picked up a handful of snow. It was light as feathers but it squeaked and crunched into a cold wet gritty ball in his palms. He threw it and hit Sasha on the shoulder.

"Stop that!" Abakar snapped. "You're not a child, what do you think you are doing? Don't be ridiculous..." And then he was spluttering around a mouthful of snow, his moustache furred with white, his eyes popping with stunned indignation. Someone laughed, high and surprised. It was Awa, laughing for the first time since she had joined them two countries ago.

Sasha threw a ball of snow at Awa. "OK, we go in. My grandmother give you tea."

The last time Adam had been inside someone's

home had been... He couldn't remember. It must have been somewhere not so far from his own home, where people with dark faces like his had sat on the bare floor, watching armed men and fires flicker across the TV screen.

Now he was in Europe, and he was amazed to find that Sasha's grandmother's house was just as small and bare. There were wooden benches around the whitewashed walls, religious pictures with big gilt frames in one corner. Most of the room was taken up with an enormous stove radiating heat. It was nothing like the houses he'd seen in magazines or films.

Sasha's grandmother crooned over Awa, taking off her snowy jacket, wrapping her in a thick, faded blanket.

"She say, how old you are?" Sasha translated. "You too young, you too thin. Why you look sad? Why you alone with all these men?"

Awa smiled at the old woman and said something not in English or Arabic, in her own language.

Sasha looked at Adam. "What she say?"

"I don't know."

Awa put her hands over the old woman's. She sounded like a different person, speaking her own language, someone much more confident, more kind. The woman chattered back incomprehensibly, words like mumbling a mouthful of sweets.

The old woman brought an old jacket leaking

wool stuffing and put it around Adam's shoulders. She patted his cheek, clucking gently, before hobbling out again.

"She's like my grandmother back home," Awa said to Adam. Her face had a soft, tender look.

"Is that who you're writing to, in your head?"

"How do you know I'm writing to someone in my head?"

"That's what I'm doing. I'm writing to my best friend, Jad. I had to leave him behind but when I get to Austria I'm going to send back money so he can come over." Adam was starting to feel comfortably drowsy. What he liked best about Awa was that she listened as if what he said mattered. "I miss him."

"My grandmother won't ever come over." Awa stared into the corner, where the big-eyed Christian saints gazed sadly from their frames. "She never travelled further than the other side of town. She wouldn't believe how far I've come." She smiled again as the old woman came back, her trembling hands holding two cracked mugs of tea. "They're all the same though, aren't they, these countries. It doesn't matter how long you travel, how far you go. Everywhere looks the same. Except for the snow."

Adam knew what she meant. All those towns, roads, people, borders. They'd blurred together into one road, the south-north, east-west highway, and everyone was either trying to get to the rich, safe north and west, or they were making money out of the people trying to go. The faces were a different colour now, the languages changed, but the money never altered, or the dreams.

"What about the rest of your family?"

Awa shrugged.

"I've got my uncle," Adam said, gloomily.

The girl slanted her eyes at Abakar, standing stiffly by the window. "He doesn't like being an illegal migrant."

"He liked being an army boss. He hates travelling with me, even though I'm the one who has to sort everything out because I know English."

Adam knew he shouldn't complain, he should be grateful. His uncle had saved and saved to pay for Adam to go to Vienna, in place of his son who'd been beaten, who'd been shot. But it was Adam's English as much as Abakar's money that had got them this far. Adam had negotiated them into buses and trucks, once on to a donkey. He had haggled and sweet-talked and lied them over more borders than he could count.

"He only treats me like a baby."

"Well, it's hard to stop being important."

"I don't know how we're going to live in Austria, me and Hand – my uncle," Adam confessed. "He thinks I'm not worth the money he spent to get me this far."

Awa looked puzzled. "You mean he is your real uncle?"

"Of course." Adam was surprised.

"A man who I called my uncle brought me out of my country," Awa said slowly. "My family paid him to be my fixer, arranging my journey. And then something went wrong and he left me in a bus station, somewhere along the way, I didn't even know which country I was in. I had to find my own way after that."

"Oh…" Now Adam finally knew why Awa was all alone, and why she never looked at the men, never talked to anyone – except him. "Oh, poor Awa…"

"I'm not poor, I am Awa; lucky. That's what my name means." She threw her head back proudly. "I'll get to where I want to be. Where are you going in Austria? Vienna?"

"My cousin Ahmed's got a greengrocer's there. And you?"

She cast him a strange sly look from the sides of her eyes. "Maybe I'll come and find you, selling fruit and veg in the West, in Vienna."

Adam looked round the little warm bare room, smelling of sour vegetables and smoke. Here, just over the border from Austria, were people living almost as he had with Jad in the refugee camp, before Abakar came for him.

O, *Jad*, he thought sleepily. *You're still back there, I hope you're there, I hope you're alive. I don't know what country I'm in, can't remember, don't care anymore. Just know it's nice to have a rest...*

The next thing he knew, he was waking up, and there was something warm and rough under his cheek. It was Awa's shoulder, still wrapped in the blanket, and as he stirred she gave him that same sly sideways look from under her lashes.

Embarrassed, he sat up. Outside the windows it was dark, and a thin, very young man, not much older than Awa, had arrived. His sharp, mean eyes raked over the five refugees.

"He say, time to go," Sasha translated. "No more wait; time is money. From you each, two hundred dollar."

Abakar was furious. "You made us wait in this hovel, and now you want us to pay so much? What for? How are you going to get us across the border?"

Ghazi hauled Abakar back. "Get a grip, man, you want to spoil everything when we're so close?"

"Two hundred dollar," Sasha repeated.

Adam sighed. Some people-smugglers were friendly, some swore at you, some ignored you, but they all wanted money. That was all there was to rely on; money in return for vague promises and half-explanations that had got them at last to this Final Border.

"We not having this money," he said. "Stupid uncle already spending it to get here."

"My brother stupid too," said Sasha. "He always want too much. I say him, you have discount, because snow. One hundred ninety."

"We not having so much." Adam knew they'd have to pay, but haggling was another law of the road.

In the end they settled on a hundred and seventy each, excavated from Ghazi's shoe, Kalif's belt, Abakar's sock. Awa went into the corner under the pictures and turned her back on them. When she came back, she was empty-handed.

"I not got enough money. I can't pay."

"No pay, no go."

"Then I don't go," she said in her clear English. "Not enough money left."

"Awa," Adam said, dismayed.

"One hundred fifty dollar," Sasha offered, hovering near the door. His brother belted him round the head, shouting impatiently.

"I not got that much."

"Then sorry. She no pay, she stay."

"We paying. Don't we?" Adam looked up at Abakar, Kalif and Ghazi in disbelief. The three men were already moving towards the door, their faces sad but resigned.

"You can't," Adam said to Awa. "Please. You must have something. We can't leave you behind too."

"Do you want to pay for me?"

Adam stared at her miserably. Inside a secret pocket of his jeans he had a hundred dollars. It was a last leaving present from Jad and his mother. Not even Abakar knew he had it. It had kept him going, when his uncle's heavy hand felt too much to bear. It was his secret hope.

"I didn't think so," Awa said. "It's all right. Take care of yourself, my friend."

As they followed Sasha down the road past the silent houses, Adam turned back to look. The little snowman had almost disappeared under the new fall of snow.

"We shouldn't have left her behind," Adam said to his uncle. "We should have helped. What'll happen to her?"

"The old woman will look after her."

"How do you know? She's all on her own."

"Be quiet!" Abakar held up that hand, his old imperious gesture, half about to make a speech, half about to strike. "You're being a baby. You have to learn, sometimes nothing can be done."

But what will she do, Jad? We left her, just the same as her fixer did. Like we didn't care at all, like she didn't matter. I'm not a baby, and there is something I can do...

He turned and began to run back as fast as he could.

"Where are you going?"

"I forgot to give the coat back," Adam called

over his shoulder.

"Adam!" His uncle's voice was thick with fury.

Adam stumbled back along the road, trying to jam his hand under the waistband of his jeans and down the left leg to the pocket sewn inside, near the knee. It was almost impossible to do this and run at the same time, but somehow he fished out the folded notes without tripping himself up. He straightened up and banged on the door.

The old woman opened it, clucking away in her chewing-sweets language.

"Awa?" Adam said.

"I'm here." Awa appeared in the doorway. "What's happened? Why have you come back?"

"Here." He thrust the folded notes into her hand and backed away quickly before he could change his mind. "It's for you."

"Adam..."

He was already running away again down the road, feeling suddenly crazily light-hearted. "See you in Vienna!" he shouted into the falling snow.

◇ ◇ ◇

The torch Sasha held was a dim, half-smothered gleam, the three men faded ghosts in the whitish darkness.

"Where did you go, man?" Ghazi hissed as he reached them. "Your uncle thought he'd lost you, he was going crazy."

"I said I'd catch up." He slunk up to his uncle. "I'm sorry."

Abakar didn't even look at him. "Don't ever do that again, you fool." His hand came down but it didn't hit him. He seized Adam's shoulder and clutched it hard.

Sasha led them off the road and into the dense trees. The snow made a delicate faint crisping and settling noise as it fell.

Didn't you always think snow was going to be warm and soft and solid, Jad? I bet you did. Well, let me tell you...

It wasn't. The flowery specks melted and soaked into the padded coat. He was wearing cheap trainers, like the others, and the icy wet seeped in and numbed his toes. As they stumbled along no detectable path, Adam started stepping in the deep holes left by his uncle's feet in the snow; it was easier than ploughing his own way.

Jad, here I am walking in the Hand's footsteps. Guess I'm going to have to put up with him a while longer. I did something stupid with your money, Jad. But I'll earn it back. I'll work hard selling fruit and veg so I can send something for you to come over and be safe too. And then you'll meet Awa, because she's going to come and find me in Vienna, she owes me, now...

He bumped into Abakar's back and almost fell

over. Sasha had clicked off the torch.

"Here," he said, "is first border."

It was a row of posts and wire between the trees. No road, no checkpoint, no guard towers, just a fence that might be to keep out cattle. That was all that marked the western border of this country.

"You climb, you quick, and you over. It easy, look..."

It took them two minutes, with Sasha leading the way.

"Where you going? You leaving your country, coming with us?"

"Everyone want to leave my country."

A few yards further the trees ended. A wide swathe of cleared earth lay ahead. There were no lights and no movement, but a faint horizontal line was sketched across the witchy paleness of the snow.

"Border of Austria." Sasha pointed.

"Why's it so quiet?" Kalif asked, after moment.

"No one cross here," Sasha said, when Adam translated. "Guards don't like snow. All inside, drinking." He held out his hand to Ghazi. "Now you on your own. I not come today." He shook hands, gravely, with Kalif and Abakar. "Maybe tomorrow."

He turned back, vanishing at once into the safe darkness of the forest.

There were no trees to hide them crossing that

swathe of white ground. But the snow fell thick as wool, wrapping them with a soft, icy, obscuring cloak as they stumbled to the Final Border. It was a ditch and a fence and a few signs in an incomprehensible language. It was harder to climb than the first had been, and Kalif tore the back of his hand open on the barbed wire. This one took perhaps five minutes for them all to reach the other side.

And that's all, Jad. That's it. No one can turn us back now. We're in Austria. Vienna's waiting for us.

"We made it," Ghazi whispered. He gave Kalif, busy nursing his cut hand, a spontaneous hug.

Adam tried to feel excited, but all he could think about was Awa and his hundred dollars. If only she'd come with them, she'd be here now, safe. And he'd know she'd be there in Vienna to help him cope with the unimaginable future, working in a fruit and veg shop in a strange country, with a cousin he hardly knew, an uncle who despised him.

The snow whirled down relentlessly. Head down, it was all he could do to keep stepping in his uncle's footsteps, one more step, one more, one more...

They were all so intent on placing one foot in front of the other that they practically walked into the soldier. He was smoking under a tree and was as surprised as they were. But he still heaved up his gun to cover them as he shouted.

"What's he saying, Adam?"

"I don't know." The black eye of the rifle pointing at them made Adam's heart jump, his mouth seize up dry. The soldier shouted again.

"Asylum," said Adam. "Refugees." His uncle's hand gripped his shoulder painfully tight. Out of somewhere his brain provided the word *"Asylsuchender"*. He'd learned that from German aid workers at home; it meant 'asylum-seeker'.

The soldier said something again that didn't sound like German.

Abakar shook Adam violently. "What is he saying?"

"I don't know!"

"Asylum,' he repeated desperately to the soldier. "Asylum here, in Austria."

"Avstria?" The soldier said it with same accent as Sasha had. He began to laugh. "Here, Austria?"

"Why is he laughing?" Ghazi demanded in bewilderment.

The soldier gestured with the rifle for them to walk, not back towards the border but further in the direction they were going. The rifle was a very old, battered AK, not what you would expect for an Austrian border guard. His round hat had earflaps; his heavy greatcoat didn't fit very well. "Avstria," he chuckled to himself, shaking his head. "Avstria…"

◇ ◇ ◇

Facing them was a desk covered with old telephones, a wall hung with faded dog-eared maps. The only new thing in the room was a glossy colour calendar with the letters UNHCR on the top. Adam recognised those letters; they stood for the United Nations High Commission for Refugees, the organisation that said he and his uncle had a right to leave their own country and claim a new life in another, safer one.

Those letters were the only thing he could understand. Ever since the soldier had led them ahead to what seemed another border, his mind had been a stupid blank. At the checkpoint the guards gave them tea and a kind of tasteless porridge. They also searched them and took away all their money. It was a poor, dirty building, smelling of cabbage and pee. The guards didn't speak English. It didn't sound like they were speaking German either. They lounged around smoking and laughing at them, thin and pimply and mean-eyed as Sasha's brother.

Kalif and Ghazi had been taken to another room. Adam felt as if he had let them down. They had relied on him to talk to the people-smugglers, to translate and haggle and lie for them, and somehow it had gone terribly wrong, but he couldn't imagine how.

"I'm sorry, uncle," he murmured. Abakar

looked at him, and Adam realised that instead of the impatience he'd always seen in his uncle's face, there was only helpless frustration. Awa had said it was hard to stop being important. Once Abakar had commanded soldiers himself. Now he was stuck in some dirty barracks, robbed and laughed at and unable to do anything about it.

Abakar blinked, and reached out to touch Adam's knee. "It's not your fault. I'm sorry I couldn't look after you, Adam."

Adam felt his eyes go wide. Before he had time to speak the door opened and an officer came in. He sat behind the desk, rubbing his eyes with one hand and lighting a cigarette with the other, and said "Well?"

Adam opened his mouth and for a terrible moment nothing came out. He couldn't remember what he had to say.

"Adam..." His uncle croaked. His face was grey with strain and fear.

Adam looked away, strangely ashamed, and the two phrases he had learned so long ago came out smooth and clear. "They will kill us if we go back. We are seeking asylum."

The officer laughed, wearily. "Not another one," he said, in good, precise English. "You don't want asylum, not here. Where do you think you are?"

"What you mean?"

"You don't know where you are, do you? You think you are in France or Germany or Italy; somewhere civilised and rich and Western."

"Austria," Adam said weakly.

The officer sat back. "There are a thousand kilometres and two more borders between here and Austria," he said, watching Adam's face. "My guard found you two kilometres away, heading for the western border of my country."

"We... we never crossing no border?" Adam felt the prickle of disbelieving tears.

"You are still in one of the poorest countries in Europe, where most people want to escape to somewhere better. You don't even know my country exists, do you? And yet my poor country has to deal with you, Yet we have to pay border guards to keep you out of rich countries, feed you and find translators and decide what to do with you. And do we get any thanks from our West European neighbours for this?"

Adam shook his head.

"We don't know where you come from, we have no money to send you back. You and your dreams." The officer stubbed his cigarette violently in an ashtray. "Most of our people have the same dream as you. Perhaps if we do a good job to keep you out of western Europe, then the European Union will let us join, and we can go there legally. Translate this for your father. Tell him we are all travelling along the same road from East to West, but we are a step closer along it than you are."

Adam stared at him, blinking the tears back. "They tricking us," he managed to stammer out at last.

"Of course they tricked you. Now tell me, your father is an army officer, a hero."

"How you knowing that?"

"They always are." The officer suddenly gave him a tired, not unkind smile. "How long you have been on the road?"

Adam shook his head again. It was a question he knew he shouldn't answer, and anyway, he didn't know the answer.

"Well, never mind. How old are you?"

"12."

"And only once in 12 years you have been tricked? Then you are lucky."

You should be so lucky, lucky lucky lucky… the idiotic song ran round in Adam's head. But it was Awa who was lucky. Lucky because she'd been left behind, and she still had a chance to find the real Final Border, that had on the other side of it a new, safe, unimaginable home.

"What is he saying, Adam?"

Adam turned to look at his uncle. There was a terrible sag to Abakar's square shoulders. Even his stiff black moustache seemed to droop. His voice was cracked with defeat.

"He says..." Adam clenched his fists. This wasn't the end of the world. Awa had been abandoned once, but she hadn't given up; he wouldn't either. "Uncle, he says we are lucky."

❖ ❖ ❖

"*Salaam.*"

The greengrocer looked up from the crate of beans. He saw a girl of perhaps 15, standing in the doorway. She was like a ray of brightness in the drab Viennese suburb, her yellow dress making her smooth black skin shine.

"Are you Ahmed? From Sudan?" she asked him in Arabic.

"Yes." He frowned suspiciously. When people asked questions like that, he still had to remind himself that there was nothing to be afraid of; he was legally in Austria.

"Do you have a cousin called Adam? And his uncle, Abakar?"

Startled, Ahmed put down the crate and gestured her inside. The street was almost deserted this October afternoon. He swung the sign on the door to 'Closed.'

"Sit down, my wife'll make us some tea."

They settled on upturned crates behind the counter.

"Is he here? Did Adam make it to Vienna?"

"Why are you asking? What do you know about it? You're not from Sudan."

She shook her head. "I travelled with Adam for a while last winter, on the way here. And then we lost each other... I made it to Vienna in December. I've just had my asylum claim approved." She took out her papers from her bag to show him.

"That's great! But Adam's not here," Ahmed said. "I heard from my uncle Abakar three months ago. He called from somewhere in Europe, I can't remember where, Moldova maybe, or was it Macedonia? They got lost in all those strange little countries. They were put on a train back east and left to find their own way." He sighed. "In Africa we were so busy with our own problems, no one ever told us Europe was so complicated."

The girl bent her head over the bag and took out a folded note.

"When they get here, please give this to Adam."

"What's this?" It looked like a hundred dollar bill.

"It's Adam's. Tell him I came to give it back."

"Wait a bit and you can tell him yourself." Ahmed thought she might be crying. "Are you all right? What's your name?"

"Awa." The girl threw back her head proudly, her eyes gleaming. "It means lucky."

"Don't go." Ahmed patted her arm, as she made to get up. "Stay and tell me about Adam. I haven't seen him since he was a little boy, but my uncle Abakar thinks the world of him."

"Do you really think he'll get here?"

Ahmed thought about the defeat he'd heard in Abakar's harsh voice over the phone, and the three months of silence since that last call. Then he held up the note and said bravely, "Of course he will, if you gave him a little of your luck in return for this. And he'll arrive even faster now you're here waiting for him."

Glossary of terms

Baa and the Angels

Ugali – a solid porridge made of ground maize, like polenta

Mzungu – a white European man or woman

Only Up From Here

Koran – the holy book of Islam

Samir Hakkim's Eating Diary

Foul medames – large brown beans

Koran – the Holy Book of Islam

Kurds – a group of people who live in northern Iraq

Shorja market – a street market in Baghdad

Tahini – a dip made from sesame seeds

Writing to the President

Mealie meal – ground corn used to make *sadza*, the staple food for Zimbabweans

Green Bombers – an unofficial militia of young men, supporters of President Mugabe. They are accused of terrorising people in Zimbabwe.

War veterans – fighters in the war for Zimbabwean independence. President Mugabe has tried to buy their support with promises of land seized from white farmers and members of the opposition.

Peri-peri – a hot red spice

NASS – National Asylum Support Service

Beans for Tea
Haram – forbidden

A Place to Hide
Dhow – an Arab boat with one mast
imam – a priest
NASS – National Asylum Support Service
Shuk – an open-air market
Three Towns – Khartoum (the capital city of Sudan), North Khartoum and Omdurman, situated close together at the junction of the White and Blue Nile.

UNDER THE WEATHER

Edited by Tony Bradman

From the effects of rising sea levels to changes in
animal behaviour and human lifestyles, these powerful
stories portray the issues surrounding climate change
in personal terms and so bring them vividly to life.
Offering warnings and inspiration in equal measure,
the stories cover a wide range of localities from
Siberia and Canada to Australia, UK, Sri Lanka
and the Philippines. Writers include award-winning
Linda Newbery as well as exciting newcomers like
Australia's George Ivanoff. Whether read from cover
to cover or dipped into for one or two stories,
this book will enlighten and inspire everyone to
consider how climate change will affect us all.